Becoming a BORDER PATROL AGENT

Becoming a

BORDER PATROL AGENT

NEW YORK

Published in the United States by LearningExpress, LLC, New York.

Library of Congress Cataloging-in-Publication Data:
Becoming a border patrol agent.—1st ed.
p. cm.
Includes bibliographical references.
ISBN-10: 1-57685-681-X
ISBN-13: 978-1-57685-681-9
1. Border patrol agents—United States. 2. Border patrol agents—Vocational guidance—United States. 3. Border patrols—United States. I. LearningExpress (Organization)
JV6483.B435 2009
363.28'502373—dc22 2008047180

Printed in the United States of America

9 8 7 6 5 4 3 2 1

Regarding the Information in This Book

Every effort has been made to ensure the accuracy of directory information up until press time. However, phone numbers and/or addresses are subject to change. Please contact the respective organization for the most recent information.

For more information or to place an order, contact LearningExpress at:
2 Rector Street
26th Floor
New York, NY 10006

Or visit us at:
www.learnatest.com

Contents

Introduction

Why You Need This Book

If you like a challenging job and want to continue serving the country [and you like being outdoors 24/7], *this is it. Your office is a car, and you're out there. You may also be on a snowmobile, an ATV, a motorcycle, a horse, whatever the environment demands. If I didn't like it, I wouldn't still be here. It's been a good run. My whole career has been in the federal government. I'm trying to coach my son into it the same way. We need more people in the society who want to serve. It's a great country we have.*

—V. Gregory Mish, Assistant Chief Patrol Agent for the U.S. Border Patrol in Buffalo, NY, who has served 26 years in the Border Patrol after 6 years in the U.S. Marine Corps

THIS BOOK describes the work and responsibilities of Border Patrol Agents. It provides information on what qualifications you need to apply to become a Border Patrol Agent, how to apply, what skills you will need to be a successful Agent, and what you will actually do once you're on the job. If you've already decided this is the right job for you, and you're ready to prepare for the Border Patrol Exam, LearningExpress's *Border Patrol Exam, Fourth Edition*, is an essential tool to use alongside this guide, and provides two complete practice tests for thorough preparation.

First, let's take a look at the official mission of the Border Patrol, essential information on who can apply, some demographic statistics of Border Patrol Agents, and some key achievements in the Border Patrol since the creation of the Department of Homeland Security in 2003.

AN OVERVIEW OF THE BORDER PATROL PROFESSION

Border Patrol Agents work for the Customs and Border Protection Agency (CBP). The Border Patrol was formerly part of the INS, the now-defunct Immigration and Naturalization Service, which was folded into the Department of Homeland Security in 2003: see Chapter 6 for a complete history of the Border Patrol. Here's the mission statement of the CBP:

> We are the guardians of our nation's borders. We are America's frontline. We safeguard the American homeland at and beyond our borders. We protect the American public against terrorists and the instruments of terror. We steadfastly enforce the laws of the United States while fostering our nation's economic security through lawful international trade and travel. We serve the American public with vigilance, integrity, and professionalism.

The CBP accomplishes these goals by performing the following duties:

- screening passengers, vehicles, and shipments entering the United States
- seizing illegal narcotics, vehicles, and agricultural products
- preventing unauthorized entry into the United States
- rescuing individuals who fall into dangerous conditions when traversing U.S. borders

Here's a quick overview of the results of those responsibilities, in (fiscal) 2006:[1]

- The Border Patrol stopped more than 1 million people from entering the United States illegally.
- The Border Patrol seized more than 1.3 million pounds of marijuana.
- The Border Patrol seized more than 13,000 pounds of cocaine.

The Border Patrol seizes more drugs per year than all other Federal agencies combined.[2] Currently, the busiest area is the Border Patrol's Tucson Sector, in Arizona.[3] Chapter 1 includes a list (Exhibit 1-4) and a map (Exhibit 1-5) of all 20 sectors.

Since the terrorist attacks of September 11, 2001, the Border Patrol's functions have changed: the agency became part of the Department of Homeland Security's U.S. Customs and Border Protection agency. Moreover, the new CBP has a new "priority mission" to prevent terrorist and terrorist weapons from entering the United States.[4] Although the primary responsibilities of a Border Patrol Agent's job are still preventing illegal aliens and illegal contraband (especially drugs) from crossing U.S. borders, this new mission placed additional pressure on Border Patrol Agents. Here's how one Border Patrol spokesman summed up the change: "We have to be not only more vigilant, we have to look for more things. We have to be concerned with trucks carrying a lot of fertilizer or individuals carrying lab equipment. Before, we wouldn't have second-guessed it. Now, we have to second-guess it."[5]

Chapter 1 provides more detailed information on the duties and responsibilities of Border Patrol Agents; Chapter 2 provides specifics on the intellectual, interpersonal, and physical skills required to become an Agent.

CAN YOU BE A BORDER PATROL AGENT? WHAT YOU NEED TO KNOW BEFORE YOU APPLY

According to www.usajobs.gov, the official job site of the U.S. Federal Government, there are several key requirements you need to meet in order to apply to become a Border Patrol Agent:

- You must be a U.S. citizen.
- You must be under the age of 40 when you apply (formerly, this age requirement was age 37).
- You must have a valid state driver's license.
- You must have lived in the United States for the last three years before you apply.
- You must take a drug test.
- You must not have been convicted of domestic violence.
- You must take a medical exam and a physical fitness exam.
- You must pass a background security investigation.

Additionally, you need to have either a college education (a four-year bachelor's degree) or one year of work experience that exposed you to stressful situations demanding quick decisions (such as police work or other law enforcement or active military duty). Chapter 1 provides details on the qualifications and work requirements for different levels of employment.

If you meet these basic requirements and are interested in learning more about Border Patrol work, this book is for you, so read on. Keep in mind, however, some sobering statistics:

- The Border Patrol recruited more than 70,000 people in a recent year to get 1,700 qualified agents.[6] *That's only about 2.5% of recruits who made the cut.* According to one agent, the hardest part of the Border Patrol application process is the stringent background check.[7]
- *Only 40% of people who apply to become a Border Patrol Agent pass the written exam* (described in Chapters 4 and 5). Todd Bryant, acting assistant chief of the Border Patrol's training and recruitment branch, says "It's a very difficult test. . . . If you come in cold [that is, without studying and preparing for the test], your chances aren't good."
- Moreover, for every 30 people who apply to take the Border Patrol's written exam (described in Chapters 4 and 5), only one person enters the Border Patrol Academy. *That's only 3.3% of all applicants.*
- Finally, there's also *a 12% attrition rate of trainees*, according to T.J. Bonner, president of the National Border Patrol Council, which is the Agents' union.[8]

Also, keep in mind that you may be rated unsuitable for a Border Patrol Agent position if your background includes any of the following:

- past or present arrests
- convictions, including misdemeanor domestic violence charges (as noted above, in the key requirements)
- dismissals from previous jobs
- debts and financial issues
- excessive use of alcohol
- use of illegal drugs, and/or the sale and distribution of illegal drugs

And you may be subject to a polygraph examination.[9]

If you've served in the military, you may find it easier to become a Border Patrol Agent, as some of the work and many of the work conditions (such as terrain and climate) are similar. There is also veterans' preference in hiring for the Border Patrol. Chapter 3 provides details on the military advantage.

The complete application process is described in detail in Chapter 4. Also, keep in mind that when the CBP is actively recruiting for agents, information will be posted on the CBP.gov website or on the USA Jobs website.

WHAT YOU NEED TO KNOW ABOUT THE BORDER PATROL ACADEMY—AN OVERVIEW

If you do get hired, you need to complete successfully a 55-day paid Basic Academy training at the U.S. Border Patrol Academy in Artesia, New Mexico. This training is described in detail in Chapter 4. If you don't speak Spanish, you will also attend an additional 40 days (beyond the 55-day basic Academy training) for Spanish language instruction.[10] This is 13 weeks (more than 3 months) of training, and training may continue for 17 weeks or even 20 weeks—in other words, 5 months. Details on the Border Patrol Academy and other education are provided in Chapter 2.

You should keep in mind that if you are accepted into the Academy, you must travel to the training in New Mexico at your own expense; you are discouraged from bringing a car or other vehicle; you are discouraged (respectfully) from bringing your family or moving your household, because there is no place to house them on the Academy campus (although your living quarters at the Academy will be provided at no cost to you, in the dorms); and you will therefore be away from your family and home for a considerable amount of time.

WHAT YOU NEED TO KNOW ABOUT THE JOB ITSELF—THE SHORT ANSWER

If you pass all your tests in the Academy and you are sent out into the field, you need to be prepared (and willing) to work overtime and perform shift work under arduous conditions. You must also maintain proficiency in the use of firearms. You will be subject to random drug testing, since one of your responsibilities is to detect and apprehend drug smugglers. You may also be sent on mandatory temporary assignments on short notice and on permanent reassignments to any duty location, so you must be ready and willing to go wherever you're needed. Finally, you should know that all Border Patrol Agents begin their careers along the Southwest border of the United States.[11] Chapter 2 describes in detail the specific responsibilities and duties of Border Patrol Agents.

DEMOGRAPHIC COMPOSITION OF THE BORDER PATROL AGENCY

There are more than 13,000 Agents working for the U.S. Border Patrol (as of July 2007, which is the most recent official count); in fiscal year 2007, the Border Patrol hired 1,000 agents, bringing the total number of agents to 13,350. That number is expected to increase by 50% in the very near future. In 2008, President George W. Bush committed to hiring 6,000 more agents by the end of the year—the biggest expansion in the Border Patrol's nearly 82-year history.[12] This is a significant increase: only once before—in 1998[13]—did the agency increase its ranks by more than 1,000 in a single year. Between 1992 and 2006, the Border Patrol increased the number of its Agents only by an average of 530 per year, growing from 4,139 to 12,084.[14] The cost of training new agents is estimated to be as much as $179,000 per agent.[15]

The CBP is an Equal Opportunity Employer, which means that all candidates are considered, regardless of race, color, religion, gender, national origin, age, sexual orientation, protected genetic information, status as a parent, lawful political affiliation, marital status, physical or mental disability (if it's not a job factor), membership or nonmembership in an employee organization, or any other nonmerit factor.

Here are some demographic statistics on who becomes a Border Patrol Agent:[16]

- As of July 2007, there were 12,967 Border Patrol Agents (as mentioned, President Bush announced a commitment to increase this number to 18,000 by the end of 2008).

- Of those 12,967 agents, 693 were women, which is only 5.4% of the Border Patrol force.
- Here's the demographic breakdown of those 693 women:
  - 398 were Hispanic women
  - 275 were Caucasian women
  - 10 were African-American women
  - 6 were Asian-American women
  - 4 were Native American women
- 19.8% of officers in the Border Patrol are women; contrast this number to other federal agencies:
  - 18.5% of FBI agents are women
  - 13.3% of ATF agents are women
  - 10.5% of Secret Service agents are women

Finally, Exhibit I-1 shows a breakdown of how many Border Patrol Agents are assigned to each type of border.

Exhibit I-1. Number of Border Patrol Agents in Various U.S. Locations

Location	as of 9/2006	as of 12/2008 (projected, as of 3/07)	increase in #	increase in %
Southwest border	11,032	15,828	4,796	43
Northern border	919	1,975	1,056	115
Coastal border	153	205	52	34
Headquarters	119	185	66	55
Other offices within the CBP	126	126	0	0
Total	12,349	18,319	5,970*	48

*Total reduced by 30 agents to account for overhires in fiscal year 2006.
Source: Report prepared by Richard M. Stana, Director of Homeland Security and Justice Issues for The Honorable Mike Rogers, Ranking Minority Member of the Subcommittee on Management, Investigations, and Oversight, the Committee on Homeland Security, and the House of Representatives: GAO-07-540R Border Patrol Training: www.gao.gov/new.items/d07540r.pdf.

STATISTICS ON ILLEGAL IMMIGRATION TO THE UNITED STATES

The United States is, of course, a country of immigrants. The first settlers came in the 1600s and 1700s, and the first great wave of immigration after that was from 1815 to 1860, when 5 million people came to this fledgling country. Approximately 150,000 people came in 1820 alone, bringing the U.S. population to about 9.5 million people. (Compare that to the 2000 census count of the population of New York City, which was about 8.2 million!) By 1880, the U.S. population had grown to more than 50 million, and more than 5.2 million immigrants arrived between 1880 and 1890—which brought the first laws restricting immigration, especially Chinese immigration (see Chapter 6 for details). Of course, those restrictions spawned a rise in *illegal* immigration. By 1900, the U.S. population reached almost 76 million, and the Mexican Revolution in 1910 caused thousands of Mexicans to flee to the United States, in search of employment.[17]

Fast-forward to the end of the twentieth century and here are just a few interesting statistics about the rise in illegal immigration to the United States:

- The number of illegal immigrants in the United States quadrupled over the last 30 years:
  - 1980: 3 million
  - 1986: 4 million
  - 1996: 5 million
  - 2000: 8.4 million[18]
  - 2007: 12.4 million[19]
- The Pew Hispanic Center estimates that 850,000 illegal immigrants have arrived in the United States every year since 2000.[20]
- The Pew Hispanic Center also reported the demographics of illegal immigrants:
  - 56% are Mexican
  - 22% more come from other Latin American countries, mainly in Central America
  - 13% (approximately) are from Asia
  - 6% are from Europe and Canada, combined[21]

- Here's a breakdown of the number of illegal immigrants, by state, as of 2006[22]:
  - California: 2.8 million (25% of the total number of illegals)
  - Texas: 1.6 million (14% of the total number)
  - Florida: 980,000 (8% of the total number)
  - Illinois: 550,000 (5% of the total number)
  - New York: 540,000 (5% of the total)
  - The next five states with the highest percentages of illegal immigrants were Arizona, Georgia, New Jersey, North Carolina, and Washington State.

In 2004, the Border Patrol stopped 1.1 million illegal immigrants from entering the United States, but critics estimated that as many as 2 million more slipped past agents because there weren't enough Border Patrol Agents to stop them.[23]

KEY ACHIEVEMENTS OF THE DEPARTMENT OF HOMELAND SECURITY

Since the Department of Homeland Security (DHS) was created following the terrorist attacks in 2001, the Border Patrol has been part of the DHS. A complete history of the Border Patrol is provided in Chapter 6, but here's a quick overview. DHS employees are responsible for protecting the territory of the United States by

- patrolling borders
- protecting ports
- defending the skies
- enforcing immigration laws
- responding to disasters and emergencies

In the first five years after it was created in 2003, the DHS has accomplished many of its goals. Some of the highlights are listed in Exhibit I-2.

Exhibit I-2. Key Achievements of the DHS from 2003 to 2008

Securing U.S. Borders

- More than 302 miles of fencing have been built.
- The number of Border Patrol Agents has increased from 10,500 (in 2003) to a target of 18,000 by the end of 2008.

Screening Travelers

- More than 2 million travelers per day are now screened.
- Secure travel documents are now required.
- More than 113 million foreign visitors' fingerprints have been checked.
- Twenty layers of screening are now performed.

Screening Ports and Cargos

- More than 97% of inbound cargo is screened for radiation at U.S. seaports.

Protecting U.S. Infrastructure

- National standards for chemical facility security and for chemicals in transit have been established.
- More than 200 actionable cyber alerts have been issued.
- Enforcing immigration laws: more than 275,000 illegal aliens have been removed.
- More than 86,000 illegal migrants at sea have been interdicted.
- Fines and judgments of more than $30 million have been secured against employers who have violated immigration laws.

Responding to Disasters

- More than 400 major disasters have been responded to.
- More than 3.78 million individuals have been helped by the DHS.

Naturalizing Citizens

- More than 2 million citizens have been naturalized between 2003 and 2006.

Countering Drug Smuggling

- More than 7 million pounds of drugs have been seized.
- More than 8,900 drug-smuggling arrests have been made on land and at sea.

So if you're interested in becoming part of the U.S. Border Patrol, turn to Chapter 1 to learn more about the profession itself, the work involved, and the salary, benefits, and career path you can expect as a Border Patrol Agent.

Becoming a BORDER PATROL AGENT

CHAPTER one

THE BASICS OF THE JOB: DUTIES, SALARY, CAREER PATH, AND HIRING TIMELINE

NOW THAT you know a little more about the CBP and its mission, about the minimum qualifications for the job and some statistics on who becomes a Border Patrol Agent, as well as some of the statistics on the problem of illegal immigration and contraband smuggling, this chapter provides more information on what Border Patrol Agents actually do—in terms of the job's duties, responsibilities, and power and authority—so that you can assess whether you think this job will be right for you. This chapter also provides basic information on the salary, benefits, and career path of the job, and provides information on how to find a Border Patrol recruiter if you're interested in talking to someone to get more specific information. Finally, the chapter provides a timeline of the entire application and hiring processes.

WHY BECOME A BORDER PATROL AGENT?

Some agents are drawn to the job because it's an opportunity for them to use their military background and experience (as Chapter 3 describes in detail). For example, one Border Patrol Agent said that he had been in the Marine Corps for five-and-a-half years and felt that the situations he would encounter would be similar and the transition from one job to the other would be fairly easy.[1] Another Border Patrol Agent was in college studying criminal justice (a path that's described in Chapter 2), when he read about opportunities with the Border Patrol. He liked the fact that he would be working outdoors, that he could be near his family, and that the benefits were very good.[2]

One trainee who had just graduated from the Border Patrol Academy applied after working in Army intelligence, and as a state narcotics agent in Mississippi. This new agent said he was attracted to the job because it would provide a good salary and a better balance between his work and his family: "I'm going to get a good paycheck out of this deal. I'm going to get my good family time. When I was with state narcotics, I was never home, so this kind of combines the best of all worlds."[3]

Another trainee said he was drawn to the Border Patrol by the opportunity to work outdoors. He had been a home loan processor for a bank in Phoenix, and one of his college professors informed him of the growing work opportunities with federal law enforcement agencies. He said, "The more I looked into it, the more I wanted to do that, get away from the desk job."[4]

Another Agent was invited to apply by a Border Patrol recruiter who thought he would be good for the job because he was a Mexican native who had become a U.S. citizen, he had served in the U.S. Army, and he was already working at a detention center for another federal immigration agency. This agent felt he would be a good fit for the Border Patrol because of the discipline he had learned in the army and because of his deep understanding of Mexican culture.[5]

The job descriptions listed on government websites are typically very straightforward. Exhibit 1-1 shows the beginning of a somewhat different ad that appeared on hotjobs.com in October 2008.

EXHIBIT 1-1. Excerpt from an Ad for Border Patrol Agents

The United States Border—Protected by You!

As a U.S. Border Patrol Agent working on America's Southwest border, you'll work with an amazing team of professionals protecting the country from terrorists, WMD, drugs, criminals and unlawful border crossings in Arizona, California, New Mexico, South Texas and West Texas.

The work is fun, challenging and critically important to national security. By protecting the border you protect the entire nation. Once you're accepted into the Border Patrol, you'll start with five months of rigorous Border Patrol Training in Artesia, New Mexico, during which you're on full salary with uniforms and equipment provided. Once you graduate, you'll head for your duty station, where a field training officer will help teach you to apply what you learned in the academy. Somewhere between a team and a family, the people you'll work with are dedicated to protecting the border and protecting each other. Here you will feel like part of something important.

Border Patrol Agents are frequently on the move, and the work will challenge you mentally and physically. Most of what you do will take place outdoors, either hiking or in one kind of vehicle or another. Your powers of observation and decision-making skills will get sharper every day. As you advance, you can train for numerous assignments and other opportunities (i.e. canine, ATV, Horse Patrol, academy instructor, etc.).

The most successful agents are the ones who reach for more. And the Border Patrol provides ample chances for agents who want to move to prove themselves, both in the field and the classroom.

See http://hotjobs.yahoo.com: search for Border Patrol Agent and Border Patrol jobs.

Although the Border Patrol may describe the job this way when recruiting, it also faces challenges with *retaining* agents: as many as 30% of new agents leave the job in the first 18 months. Why? Here's another way of looking at the same job description: "Law enforcement officers wanted: must work graveyard shifts alone in remote towns along the Mexican border, put in long hours, and perform well in triple-digit temperatures."[6] The CBP recognizes this problem, but obviously there's nothing it can do about the climate or terrain conditions, except to prepare applicants and trainees for what to expect.

WHAT BORDER PATROL AGENTS DO: AN OVERVIEW

Essentially, Border Patrol Agents monitor U.S. land borders, primarily in Texas, New Mexico, Arizona, and California, which are the four states where the U.S. borders Mexico, but also on the Northern border with Canada and along the U.S. coastline and ports of entry. These borders span a lot of miles:[7]

- There are 6,000 miles of Mexican and Canadian land borders (almost 2,000 of which is the Mexican border).
- There are 2,000 miles of coastal waters surrounding the Florida Peninsula and the island of Puerto Rico.

This is rigorous work, and you will need to know how to monitor a border, and how to drive in high-speed and off-road situations. You'll need to know about immigration law and government ethics to do your job effectively, how to fire handguns and assault rifles, how to find cover in hostile situations, how to make judgment calls on when to use deadly force, and even how to search moving trains for stowaways.

Border Patrol Agents are part of the U.S. Customs and Border Protection Agency; here's how the CBP describes the key duties and responsibilities of border patrol agents:

> The primary focus of Border Patrol Agents is to work in tandem with U.S. Customs and Border Protection (CBP) partners to prevent terrorists and terrorist weapons from entering the United States. Border Patrol Agents also detect and prevent the smuggling and unlawful entry of undocumented aliens into the United States and apprehend people found to be in violation of U.S. immigration laws. Additionally, due to the increase in drug smuggling operations, they are the primary drug-interdicting agents along the land borders.[8]

The CBP goes on to describe one of the most important duties performed by Border Patrol Agents, which is known as *line-watch*. This involves the detection and apprehension of undocumented aliens and their smugglers. In other words, if you're a Border Patrol Agent doing line-watch, you may be doing all of the following:

- maintaining surveillance from a covert position
- pursuing leads
- responding to electronic sensor alarms
- utilizing infrared scopes during night operations
- using low-light level television systems
- sighting aircraft
- interpreting and following tracks, marks, and other physical evidence

Border Patrol Agents also perform traffic checks, traffic observation, city patrol transportation checks, and other administrative, intelligence, and anti-smuggling activities (described in the next section of this chapter).

Border Patrol work entails many hazards, involving not only people, but also vehicles, firearms, and various physical environments. Border Patrol Agents must constantly be alert to hostile and unpredictable behavior by people they have apprehended for suspected violations of immigration, customs, or narcotics laws. Agents often deal with dangerous criminals who are in the act of fleeing arrest or who are carrying narcotics or other contraband, and Border Patrol Agents must react instantly to threats of harm to themselves and/or to others. Additionally, Border Patrol Agents often need to operate automobiles in high-speed chases in order to try to stop fleeing vehicles. Finally, Border Patrol Agents typically work in extreme climates and extremely difficult terrains, both of which present hazardous conditions.

ASSESSING WHETHER YOU WANT THE JOB

If this brief description sounds interesting to you, take the self-assessment questionnaire shown in Exhibit 1-2. This is a series of questions the Transportation Security Administration (TSA) offers on the following website: www.tsa.gov/assets/pdf/soar/bpa_self_assessment_tool.pdf.

EXHIBIT 1-2. Self-Assessment Questionnaire for Prospective Border Patrol Agent Applicants

First, ask yourself: "Would I enjoy . . ."	*YES*	*NO*
1. work that involves physical and mental challenges?		
2. work that is adventuresome, exciting, and rewarding?		
3. forming lifelong friendships with an elite group of people?		
4. learning about and living in new and different cultures?		
5. working in an organization known for its intense camaraderie and loyalty?		
6. working on a team?		
7. working outdoors?		
8. performing a job that protects the United States from threats to its people and way of life—including terrorists, terrorist weapons, and illegal drugs?		
9. encountering and arresting illegal aliens and smugglers of aliens?		
10. using a variety of high-tech equipment (such as night-vision goggles, ATVs, unmanned aerial vehicles, aircraft, etc.) and weapons?		
11. having a career that is more a way of life than a job?		

Next, ask yourself: "Would I be willing to . . ."	*YES*	*NO*
1. work irregular and unscheduled hours and overtime, including shift work, weekends, nights and holidays, and—at times—away from my permanent duty station?		
2. wear a prescribed uniform and conform to established grooming standards?		
3. attend a rigorous five-month physical and academic training program that will be away from my current residence?		
4. travel for conferences, training, or special operations?		
5. execute orders or follow policies that may conflict with my personal or religious beliefs?		
6. encounter aliens suffering poverty or extreme hardship, or carrying infectious diseases, or witness drowning, vehicle accidents, and other tragedies?		

EXHIBIT 1-2. Continued

YES *NO*

7. be exposed to all kinds of weather and environmental and hazardous conditions even when wearing protective equipment?
8. work alone in remote areas for extended periods of time, including throughout the night, when I may have limited communication risk and be at high of danger?
9. live in remote locations that may have limited conveniences, such as housing, schools, healthcare, and entertainment?

Finally, ask yourself: "Could I meet the following requirements . . ." *YES* *NO*

1. qualify with, carry, and maintain proficiency in the use of firearms?
2. never have been convicted of a crime of violence?
3. be able and willing to use deadly force (e.g., firearm) to protect my life, the lives of fellow officers, or the lives of innocent bystanders if I found myself in a life-threatening situation?
4. be able to engage in strenuous physical exertion, such as heavy lifting, crouching or crawling in restricted areas, climbing, and running?
5. by the time referred for selection, be a U.S. citizen (and have lived in the United States for the last three years) with a valid driver's license and be under the age of 40 (unless I'm currently serving or formerly served in a Federal civilian law enforcement retirement-covered position)?
6. learn Spanish (if I don't already know it)?
7. pass a security background check?
8. pass a medical/physical examination?
9. pass initial and random drug tests?

If you answered ***YES*** to most or all of the questions, that is a good indication that becoming a Border Patrol Agent could be the right career for you.

If you answered ***NO*** to a lot of the questions, you should think carefully about your decision at this time to apply for a BPA position. Fortunately, there are other careers at the Department of Homeland Security that may be more to your liking, so you may want to visit the Department's website at http://www.dhs.gov/xabout/carers/index.shtm.

OBJECTIVES AND AUTHORITY OF BORDER PATROL AGENTS

The U.S. Border Patrol and the Agents who work for this agency have a long list of objectives:

1. to detect and prevent aliens from entering the United States illegally
2. to detect and apprehend people who are smuggling aliens, narcotics, and other contraband into the United States
3. to locate, identify, and apprehend aliens who are already illegally in the United States
4. to apprehend Immigration Law violators, many of whom may be U.S. citizens or lawful permanent residents (in addition, Border Patrol Agents can apprehend such violators *with or without* warrant)
5. to identify and establish factual information pertaining to fraudulent claims of U.S. citizenship
6. to identify and apprehend people who produce, sell, or possess documents—whether the documents are counterfeit, fraudulent, or genuine—that are purposefully being used to circumvent the laws of the United States
7. to deal with alleged violators in any of the above situations by establishing a prima facie case (that is, a case that seems to be self-evident from the facts provided) and to properly dispose of individual cases in one of the following ways:
    - ▷ referring the alleged violator for a formal administrative hearing
    - ▷ detaining the alleged violator for further identification and interrogation
    - ▷ detaining the alleged violator for criminal prosecution in Federal court
    - ▷ referring the alleged violator for a formal deportation or exclusion hearing
    - ▷ referring the case to another agency
    - ▷ releasing the alleged violator or arranging for voluntary departure under safeguards, as appropriate
8. to prepare reports that are clear, concise, comprehensive, and accurate—and to work to minimize errors in or omissions of factual matters used to prepare those reports

9. to improve the effectiveness of Federal law enforcement when serving as a prosecution or expert witness in Federal court

To fulfill these obligations, Border Patrol Agents have specific power and authority, which is very clearly described by the U.S. Office of Personnel Management (OPM): see Exhibit 1-3.

EXHIBIT 1-3. Power and Authority of Border Patrol Agents

After establishing probable cause and the presence of an articulable fact, (a fact capable of being expressed clearly) Border Patrol Agents may, without warrant, exercise judiciously the following powers:

1. interrogate any alien or person believed to be an alien about his or her right to be in or remain in the United States
2. arrest any alien who, in their presence or view, is entering or attempting to enter the United States in violation of law
3. arrest any alien in the United States in violation of law if there is likelihood of escape before a warrant can be obtained
4. board vessels and other conveyances to search for aliens
5. enter private lands within a distance of 40 kilometers (25 miles) of any external boundary for purposes of patrolling the borders of the United States to prevent the illegal entry of aliens
6. make arrests for felonies which have been committed and which are cognizable under any law regulating the admission, exclusion, or expulsion of aliens if there is reason to believe the person is guilty of such felony and is likely to escape before a warrant of arrest can be obtained
7. conduct a search of the person and of the personal effects in the possession of any person seeking admission to the United States

Border Patrol Agents are also empowered to execute warrants and other processes issued by any officer under laws regulating the admission, exclusion, or expulsion of aliens. Furthermore, they are empowered to administer oaths and to take and consider evidence concerning the privileges of any person to enter, re-enter, pass through, or reside in the United States, or concerning any matter which is material or relevant to the enforcement of the immigration and nationality laws and the administration of the Immigration and Naturalization Service. Border Patrol Agents are cross-designated to enforce Title 18 and Title 21 laws.

Source: "Position Classification Standard for Border Patrol Agent Series, GS-1896," U.S. Office of Personnel Management, page 6, www.opm.gov/fedclass/gs1896.pdf.

BASIC DUTIES OF BORDER PATROL AGENTS

The OPM provides general information on the duties and responsibilities of a Border Patrol Agent. These are described in the following sections.[9]

International Boundary Security Control Operations. Here, you will be working at or near a land border or a coastline. You will maintain a general surveillance over your assigned area by observing the people and events in that area and by questioning persons, if and when necessary. You may also *lie in* (the U.S. government's term) at selected strategic points along the border you are watching, and you may intercept illegal entrants (who may then be detained or expelled from the United States).

Sign Cutting. Here, you will also be working at or near a land border or a coastline; however, this work requires you to visually detect and interpret tracks, marks, and other physical evidence left by people, animals, or vehicles, or other objects that have been moving through the area you are watching. This work also involves identifying and apprehending illegal aliens and smugglers of narcotics or other contraband who enter or pass through the area you are watching.

Farm and Ranch Check. This work consists of systematically checking farms, ranches, lumber camps, and other potential employers of laborers and other unskilled or semi-skilled workers. You will be looking for illegal aliens who have escaped detection at U.S. borders or who have violated their immigration status, and if you find any, you will arrange for them to be detained, deported, or depart voluntarily from the United States.

Traffic and Transportation Check. This work consists of establishing and maintaining traffic checkpoints on roads or highways, in order to intercept and inspect cars and trucks that may be transporting illegal aliens and smugglers from U.S. borders into the interior of the United States. It also involves interrogating the occupants of these vehicles regarding their immigration status in the United States—and this interrogation goes beyond just the driver: you may also interrogate anyone already on board or who are boarding buses, trains, airplanes, or any other conveyance. In some areas of the country, traditional traffic check activities have been eliminated or curtailed by court actions, so you must know the laws that apply in the area you are watching, and you may need to secure and periodically justify and renew warrants of inspection in order to continue your traffic check responsibilities.

City Patrol. This work involves looking for deportable aliens who are attempting to assimilate into the community. To do this, you will systematically check local industries, businesses, hotels, rooming houses, construction projects, camps, parks, jails, and other public institutions where deportable aliens are likely to be working or living. This work is often coordinated with other law enforcement agencies at the federal, state, and local level.

Boat Patrol. For this type of work, you will patrol coastal and other boundary waters, looking for deportable aliens. You will need to operate various types of marine patrol craft to do so. You may board small boats, including pleasure boats, commercial fishing, boats, shrimp boats, and tugboats.

Crew Control. Here, you will patrol waterfronts, to check for crew who have been detained on ships, to search vessels to prevent desertion of crew; to prevent stowaways from landing, and to locate and arrest any aliens who have entered the U.S. illegally. To do this work effectively and successfully, you need to establish and maintain good relationships with ships' captains, agents, shipyard and dock workers, and others who are knowledgeable about shipping activities, ships' crews, schedules, ports visited, and other related activities.

Remote Monitored Sensor System Operations. Here, you need to have a thorough knowledge of the area to which you'll be assigned, so that you can implant and camouflage remote-monitored electronic sensors, in order to detect and intercept aliens who are attempting to enter the United States illegally.

Anti-Smuggling Operations. This work involves identifying and apprehending individuals or groups who are attempting to smuggle illegal aliens into the United States (either for their own profit or not), or who are assisting aliens to enter the country illegally, or the aliens themselves who are attempting to enter illegally. In order to identify and apprehend these individuals or groups, you may need to enlist, work with, and control confidential informants.

Intelligence Operations. Here, you need to work with a wide variety of sources, including both foreign and domestic contacts, to collect strategic and tactical intelligence regarding the illegal entry or smuggling of aliens into the United States. In addition to collecting this intelligence, you need to refine, evaluate, and use it effectively. Your sources may include (but are not limited to) the following:

- other Border Patrol Agents
- other Service personnel
- Service reports
- state and local law enforcement agencies
- court officials
- private citizens
- schools
- social agencies
- civic groups
- business groups

Liaison Activities. This work requires you to establish, maintain, and improve productive liaisons with other law enforcement and administrative officials, at the federal, state, and local levels and even in foreign agencies. As necessary, you may lead or participate in cooperative coordinated activities, such as checks or raids in areas where illegal aliens gather or reside.

ESSENTIAL SKILLS AND ABILITIES

To perform all the duties and responsibilities just described, Border Patrol Agents need good judgment and various skills and abilities. Specifically, as a Border Patrol Agent, you need to be able to do all of the following:

- work effectively with informants who can provide you with necessary information regarding illegal aliens or smugglers, by developing relationships with informants, evaluating their trustworthiness and reliability, and using their services advantageously
- interrogate witnesses
- search records

- perform surveillance
- follow up on information provided by others (including informants and other law enforcement officers)
- know and be able to speak a foreign language (as noted, proficient to fluent Spanish is required for all Border Patrol Agents: requirements for fluency depends on the level of Border Patrol Agent—GS-5 agents are often just starting to learn and study Spanish, whereas GS-9 agents need to be completely fluent)
- understand foreign cultures and customs
- interact effectively with people from all walks of life, including those of different cultural backgrounds
- use (and maintain through proper care of) a variety of electronic equipment, including:
  - two-way radios
  - night scopes
  - remote-monitored sensor systems, which are used to detect and intercept aliens who are entering the United States illegally
- operate two- and four-wheel-drive vehicles, as well as other types of mobile equipment (this is why all Border Patrol Agents must have a valid driver's license; also, as noted above, some Border Patrol Agents conduct boat patrol, which requires them to be able to operate various types of marine craft)

Chapter 2 provides details on the skills and abilities you need to succeed as a Border Patrol Agent.

SALARY AND BENEFITS

The annual salary of an entry-level Border Patrol Agent ranges from $36,500 to $46,500, depending on the level at which you enter; there are three possibilities, depending on your qualifications:

- At the GS-5 level, the annual salary is $36,658 (or higher, depending on the location of the position).

- At the GS-7 level, the annual salary is $41,729 (or higher, depending on the location of the position).
- At the GS-9 level, the annual salary is $46,542 (or higher, depending on the location of the position).

You can advance from a GS-5 or a GS-7 or a GS-9 entry-level position to the GS-11 full-performance level without having to reapply, and the annual salary for a GS-11 position starts at $54,494. Moreover, once you reach the GS-11 level—which can take as little as three years—you can earn as much as $70,000 per year (including overtime, holiday, and night pay).

Border Patrol Agents receive annual increases in salary, and there is additional compensation (from 10% to 25%) for overtime work. Also, Border Patrol Agents receive a uniform allowance (of $1500) to offset the cost of purchasing the required BPA uniform. The funds are deposited into an account that each agent draws from when purchasing the uniform. Interestingly, the Border Patrol uniform changed in 2007: since the 1950s, the uniform had been more like a police officer's uniform, but in August 2007, the uniform was changed to look more like military fatigues. It now consists of lightweight cargo pants, nylon belts (instead of leather) with quick-release plastic buckles (instead of brass buckles). Also, there are two large pockets with Velcro flaps that can hold MREs (*meals ready to eat*), flashlight batteries, and GPS devices. The identifying patches (badges and nameplates) are now sewn onto the uniform, replacing the pins formerly used, which often fell off and which shone in the moonlight or other lights, making it difficult for agents to stay undercover. The uniform was changed to make it more appropriate and *more operational*, *more tactical* for the rugged terrain in which Border Patrol Agents typically work—remote mountains and deserts—and in the extreme heat climate conditions.[10]

Border Patrol Agents receive the following benefits:

- personal leave days for vacation, illness, and family care
- a wide range of health insurance programs
- life insurance
- longterm care insurance

- flexible spending accounts for out-of-pocket medical expenses or the costs of taking care of a dependent child or parent
- a retirement plan that includes a 401(k) thrift savings plan

Border patrol agents may voluntarily retire at any age after completing 25 years of service or at age 50 or older with 20 years of service. The mandatory retirement age is 57 with 20 years of service. However, if you have fewer than 20 years of service by age 57, you may work beyond the age of 57 and retire when you meet the combination of age and service requirements—although since you need to be under the age of 40 when you apply, this will likely be only another three years, unless the law changes during the years you are working.

WHAT YOUR CAREER PATH MIGHT LOOK LIKE

There are several levels of Border Patrol Agent, including the GS-5, GS-7, GS-9, GS-11, and higher levels that come with promotions once on the job. In general, Border Patrol Agents receive promotions from one GS level to the next after performing satisfactorily for one year at each grade level. There is a two-year intern program that serves as your probationary period after you become a Border Patrol Agent. The following sections describe the differences between each grade level.

If you do not have the work experience described in each of the following sections, you can still qualify to become a Border Patrol Agent at the GS-5 level, provided you have four academic years above high school leading to a bachelor's degree, or a bachelor's degree from an accredited college. And you may qualify at the GS-7 level if you have at least one full year of graduate education in law or in a field related to law enforcement, such as criminal justice or police science; you may also qualify at the GS-7 level if you meet the provisions of Superior Academic Achievement (SAA); see http://www.opm.gov/qualifications/SEC-II/s2-e5.asp for more detailed information on SAA.[11] Also, see Appendixes A and B for a complete list all U.S. accredited colleges offering criminal justice and law-enforcement programs.

Your grade level will be determined based on the information provided in your application. However, note that if you are offered and accept a position as a BPA at the GS-5 or GS-7 level, *your grade level cannot be changed after you have entered on duty.*

GS-5 Level. This is the entry level for Border Patrol Agents. In other words, you are a trainee. To qualify at this level, you must have a substantial background of work experience, and at least one year of that experience must have been comparable in level of difficulty and responsibility to grade GS-4 in the Federal service. Essentially, that means you must be able to do all three of the following:

1. take charge, make sound decisions, and maintain composure in stressful situations
2. learn law-enforcement regulations, methods, and techniques through classroom training and/or on-the-job instruction
3. gather factual information through questioning, observation, and examination of documents and records.[12]

If you are hired at the GS-5 level, you will receive formal classroom training and on-the-job experience in order to

- familiarize you with immigration and nationality laws and related rules and regulations
- familiarize you with the statutory authority of Border Patrol Agents
- familiarize you with other activities relevant to immigration law enforcement
- provide orientation on the program, policies, and procedures of the CBP, as well as its management and operational activities
- become proficient in the Spanish language
- perform such duties as sign cutting, city patrol, traffic check, and others.[13]

As mentioned earlier in this chapter, the annual salary at the GS-5 level starts at $36,658 (or higher, depending on the location to which you are assigned).

GS-7 Level. To qualify at this level, you need to have one year of law-enforcement experience comparable in level of difficulty and responsibility to the GS-5 level in the Federal service. You must demonstrate the ability to do all four of the following:

1. make arrests and exercise sound judgment in the use of firearms
2. deal effectively with individuals or groups of persons in a courteous, tactful manner in connection with law-enforcement matters
3. analyze information rapidly and make prompt decisions or take prompt and appropriate law-enforcement action in light of applicable laws, court decisions, and sound law-enforcement matters
4. develop and maintain contact with a network of informants.[14]

If you are hired or promoted to work at the GS-7 level, your duties will include enforcing the immigration and nationality laws. You will also apprehend violators of these and other related laws within the jurisdiction of the CBP. At this job level, here is essentially what you will do:

- You will detect individuals suspected of violating immigration laws, by following up on leads, personally observing people, and using other means. You will also question these people and inspect their documents to determine either their U.S. citizenship or their alien status, using Spanish, as needed, to communicate.
- You will search for persons in vehicles, buildings, and outdoor areas, and observe and interpret physical signs of illegal entry into the United States.
- You will apprehend and search violators, question them and others involved (such as witnesses), and recommend to your team leader or supervisor that suspect(s) be held for further questioning or if he/she/they should be returned immediately to the country of origin.
- You will write reports concerning apprehensions, interrogations, and other activities relevant to immigrant law enforcement.[15]

As mentioned earlier in this chapter, the annual salary at the GS-7 level starts at $41,729 (or higher, depending on the location to which you are assigned).

GS-9 Level. To qualify at this level, your experience must include the following tasks:

1. develop cases and conduct interviews or interrogations, apprehensions, and arrests in order to further the process or cease development
2. prepare cases and appear as a professional witness in court
3. exercise sound judgment in the use of firearms and conduct training, qualification exercises, or courses in the proper care and use of firearms
4. deal effectively with individuals or groups of persons in a courteous and tactful manner in their detention, control, or interrogation, and work to promote effective community outreach programs and public relations
5. analyze and disseminate intelligence information and data rapidly, and apply a practical knowledge of the laws, concepts, operational practices, and law-enforcement methods and techniques in order to independently perform duties typically encountered in law enforcement
6. develop and maintain contact with a network of informants, social and political organizations, state and local enforcement agencies, and private citizens, to ensure continuity of enforcement work and to carry out enforcement responsibilities
7. use a variety of law-enforcement databases and information retrieval systems, such as TECS, NCIC, and NEXUS (these are discussed in more detail in Chapter 4)
8. prepare reports and write other documents that deal with the collection, protection, and recording of evidence, the presentation of testimony, and the retention of informational materials concerning illegal activities and practices encountered during daily activities.[16]

Once you are working at the GS-9 level, you will be performing the full range of Border Patrol duties independently. In other words, you will be responsible for all of the following tasks.

- You will work alone or as a member of a team to perform a variety of typical duties, including these (described in detail earlier in this chapter):
  - sign cutting
  - farm and ranch check

  - ▷ traffic check
  - ▷ transportation check
  - ▷ city patrol
  - ▷ boat patrol
  - ▷ crew control
  - ▷ international boundary security operations
- You will develop and use information from a variety of sources (including informants, state and local law-enforcement agencies, social and political organizations, and private citizens) to apprehend smugglers—that is, persons who for gain assist aliens to enter the United States illegally and transport them to interior centers of population.
- You will identify individuals suspected of violating immigration laws, by following up on leads, by personal observation of persons, and by other means. You will also question these persons and inspect their documents to determine their citizenship or alien status, using Spanish as needed to communicate. You will determine their country of origin.
- You will apprehend and search violators and question them and others involved (such as witnesses). You will transport suspects to headquarters for further questioning, or you will arrange for their return to their country of origin. You will also prepare reports regarding these apprehensions, interrogations, and other related matters.
- You will use remote-monitored sensor systems and other electronic equipment (such as a nightscope) to detect and identify aliens or other persons who are entering the United States illegally.[17]

As mentioned earlier in this chapter, the annual salary at the GS-9 level starts at $46,542 (or higher, depending on the location to which you are assigned).

GS-11 Level. At this level, you will be responsible for operating and coordinating an intelligence program and for providing advance intelligence information about attempts of persons to enter the United States illegally (including alien smuggling), throughout an assigned area, typically an entire sector (see Exhibit 1-5, at the end of this chapter, for a map of all 20 Border Patrol sectors). This work involves the following responsibilities.

- You will collect intelligence information continuously, from a wide variety of sources, including these:
  - informants in the local area and in neighboring countries
  - reports from Border Patrol Agents throughout your assigned area
  - sources in other Border Patrol sectors
  - sources in other law-enforcement agencies
  - court officials
  - schools
  - welfare agencies
  - civic and business groups
- You will evaluate this intelligence information and prepare reports identifying trends and patterns in activities relating to illegal actions of aliens.
- You will use intelligence information to prepare forecasts of smuggling activities and illegal entries, and you will recommend action to counteract and apprehend violators.
- You will work in conjunction with anti-smuggling agents, as necessary, and provide expertise on fraudulent documents and other intelligence information to be used in developing smuggling cases.
- You will provide authoritative information concerning the types of counterfeit documents used in conjunction with illegal alien activities, including methods of detection, sources, and patterns of usage and distribution. You will also maintain current and complete indexes of
  - smugglers
  - smuggling activities and methods
  - informants and other sources of information
  - vendors of counterfeit and altered documents and their activities and methods of operation
  - public and private airstrips
- You will coordinate the intelligence work of other Border Patrol Agents within your assigned area, and you will train and orient lower-grade agents, as required.
- You will prepare reports concerning apprehensions, interrogations, and other pertinent matters.[18]

As mentioned earlier in this chapter, the annual salary for a GS-11 position starts at $54,494.

HOW TO LOCATE A BORDER PATROL RECRUITER

If you are interested in talking to someone about applying to become a Border Patrol Agent, or if you have questions about any aspect of the application process or the work itself, you can contact a Border Patrol recruiter. Exhibit 1-4 lists all of the sector offices of the Border Patrol Agency, the city and state where each is located, and phone numbers for all (and e-mail addresses for some offices). Exhibit 1-5 is a map of all 20 sector offices comprising the Office of Border Patrol.

Exhibit 1-4. Contact Information for Border Patrol Recruiters

Sector Office	Location	Contact Information
Blaine Sector	Blaine, WA	360-332-1610
Buffalo Sector	Grand Island, NY	1-866-775-6270 bunrecruiting@dhs.gov
Del Rio Sector	Del Rio, TX	1-888-590-2559
Detroit Sector	Detroit, MI	dtmrecruitment@cbp.dhs.gov
El Centro Sector	El Centro, CA	760-335-5900
El Paso Sector	El Paso, TX	915-834-8848
Grand Forks Sector	Grand Forks, ND	701-775-6654
Havre Sector	Havre, MT	montanaborderpatrol@dhs.gov
Houlton Sector	Houlton, ME	1-866-231-5434
Laredo Sector	Laredo, TX	956-764-3676
Marfa Sector	Marfa, TX	432-837-6120 1-888-536-6204
Rio Grande Valley Sector	Edinburg, TX	956-289-4800
Miami Sector	Miami, FL	954-965-6300

(Continued)

Exhibit 1-4. Continued

Sector Office	Location	Contact Information
New Orleans Sector	New Orleans, LA	504-376-2800
Ramey Sector	Aquadilla, PR	787-882-3561 ext. 2121 787-882-3562 ext. 2119
San Diego Sector	San Diego, CA	619-216-4211
Spokane Sector	Spokane, WA	509-353-2747 ProtectUS@dhs.gov
Swanton Sector	Swanton, VT	1-866-240-8354 802-868-5167
Tucson Sector	Tucson, AZ	520-748-3191
Yuma Sector	Yuma, AZ	928-341-6519

From www.cbp.gov/xp/cgov/caeers/customs_careers/border_careers/bp_agent/border_pocs.xml.

Exhibit 1-5. Map of the 20 Sectors Comprising the Office of Border Patrol

From www.cbp.gov/linkhandler/cgov/careers/customs_careers/border_careers/bp_agent/sectors_map.ctt/Sectors_Map.pdf.

AN OVERVIEW AND TIMELINE OF THE APPLICATION AND HIRING PROCESS

It can take five to eight months from the time you apply for a position as Border Patrol Agent to the time when you're hired and depart for your training at the U.S. Border Patrol Academy. Here's an overview and a timeline of the hiring process.

- **Step 1: Apply via the Internet.** Chapter 4 describes the online application process in detail and provides the web site URL for applying.

  Timeframe: Any time. You can apply online 24 hours a day, 7 days a week, whenever you have access to a computer and the Internet.
- **Step 2: Schedule your written test.** You will be asked to do this while you are completing the online application, and the system will offer you three choices of dates on which to take the written exam. Choose a date, and you're all set.

  Timeframe: This date should be three to eight weeks from the date you are applying online. You may want to schedule the test as late as possible, to give yourself more time to prepare for the written test, which is the next step in the application and hiring process.
- **Step 3: Prepare for the written test.** Chapter 5 describes the three tests that comprise the U.S. Border Patrol Agent test (a logical reasoning test, which all applicants take; and either a Spanish Language Proficiency Test or an Artificial Language Test: depending on your command of Spanish, you will take one or the other of these). Chapter 5 also describes the type of questions you will be asked, and refers you to other sources, publications, books, and websites that can provide you with additional guidance on the test, including practice questions with correct answers and explanations of the correct answer and why the other response choices are incorrect.

  Timeframe: As much time as you have available to prepare for the test, in the weeks before you are scheduled to take it.
- **Step 4: Wait for the results of your written test.** Some test locations are *compressed testing* locations (see Chapter 4 for details), where applicants can receive their Notice of Results (NOR) from the written test immediately. If you do not take the written test at one of

these compressed testing locations, you will receive your NOR in the mail within approximately two weeks after you take the written test. The NOR will tell you whether or not you passed the written test.

Timeframe: Either the same day you take the test (for compressed testing) or within about two weeks afterward (for all other testing).

- **Step 5: Schedule your oral interview and fitness and medical tests.** If you pass the written test, you will also receive at that time a tentative selection packet of information. You will also be scheduled for an oral board interview and for your fitness and medical tests (both of which are described in detail in Chapter 4).

  Timeframe: Four to ten weeks. If you take the written test at a compressed testing location, you will receive your tentative selection packet the same day on which you are tested, and your oral board interview and your fitness and medical tests will be scheduled within the next four weeks. On the other hand, if you take the written test at one of the other nationwide locations that does not offer compressed testing, you will receive your tentative selection packet approximately six weeks from the date you passed your written test, and your fitness and medical tests and oral board interview will be scheduled within four weeks from that time. For example,

  - if you take the test at a regular testing location on October 1,
  - you may receive your tentative selection packet on November 15,
  - and you may be scheduled for an oral board interview and your fitness and medical tests on December 15.

- **Step 6: Attend your scheduled oral board interview.** The oral board interview is given by three Border Patrol Agents. The interview does not test or require any technical knowledge; instead, it consists of situational questions that are intended to assess your judgment and decision making, your emotional maturity, your interpersonal skills, and your cooperativeness and sensitivity to the needs of others—all of which are qualities that are critical to successful performance as a Border Patrol Agent. The oral board interview is rated on a pass or fail basis, and you must receive a *pass* in all areas in order to continue to be considered in the hiring process.

  Timeframe: Within four to six weeks after receiving your tentative selection packet.

- **Step 7: Schedule and complete all other tests.** If you pass the oral board interview, you must undergo the following:
  - a drug test
  - a medical examination
  - the fitness test (see Chapter 4 for details on the fitness test)
  - a background investigation

  Timeframe: These will be scheduled and completed as soon as possible.
- **Step 8: Start work—as soon as a position becomes available.** If you successfully complete all of the above steps and tests, your name will be placed in a pipeline for a position as vacancies become available in your preferred geographic location (which you indicated during the online application process in Step 1; see Chapter 4 for details). At that time, you will receive a firm offer of employment.

  Timeframe: As soon as a position becomes available.

CHAPTER two

THE SKILLS, PHYSICAL ABILITIES, AND EDUCATION YOU NEED

CHAPTER 1 provided the basic information about the minimum requirements you need even to be considered for a job as a Border Patrol Agent, and it described what you'll be doing if you get the job. This chapter describes the specific skills, physical abilities, and education you need for the job, as well as the education and training you will receive at the Border Patrol Academy. Keep in mind, though, how one senior agent has described the work: "It's a hard job to get and a hard job to keep and we want it that way," according to Robert W. Gilbert, the Chief of the Border Patrol's Tucson Sector.[1]

REQUIRED SKILLS: AN OVERVIEW

Border Patrol Agents are required to have certain competencies, in five major areas:

1. thinking skills
2. personal characteristics
3. interacting with others
4. work management skills
5. physical and psychomotor skills

Exhibit 2-1 provides an overview of these skills, and the first part of this chapter provides a detailed look at what's required for each area.

EXHIBIT 2-1. Skills Required to Become a Border Patrol Agent

Thinking Skills

1. reasoning skills
2. decision-making skills
3. problem-solving skills
4. judgment
5. learning
6. reading

Personal Characteristics

7. conscientiousness
8. integrity/honesty
9. emotional maturity
10. cooperativeness/sensitivity to the needs of others

EXHIBIT 2-1. Continued

11. self-presentation
12. flexibility

Interacting with Others

13. writing
14. oral communication and listening
15. leadership
16. teaching others
17. negotiating
18. teamwork

Work Management Skills

19. technology application
20. organizational and community awareness
21. managing and organizing information
22. self-management
23. managing resources
24. managing human resources
25. planning and evaluating

Physical and Psychomotor Skills

26. eye–hand coordination
27. physical strength and agility
28. stamina

THINKING SKILLS

Border Patrol Agents need to have certain types of thinking skills, which the U.S. government breaks down into the following six skill sets.

1. ***Reasoning Skills.*** You need to be able to discover or select rules, principles, or relationships between facts and other information. You also need to be able to draw correct inferences from available information. And you need to be able to understand the relationships between related statements and draw the appropriate conclusions.
2. ***Decision-Making Skills.*** You also need to make sound and well-informed decisions, and to perceive the impact and implications of your decisions and other people's decisions. You need to be able to commit to action in uncertain situations in order to accomplish organizational goals. And you need to be able to effect change.
3. ***Problem-Solving Skills.*** You need to be able to identify and analyze problems. You need to be able to gather, interpret, and evaluate information in order to determine whether it is accurate and relevant to the situation you're facing. And you need to be able to use sound judgment to generate and evaluate alternatives and to recommend a solution to the problem you're facing.
4. ***Judgment.*** You need to be able to make sound decisions in situations when multiple options are available. And you need to use common sense to avoid actions that could put you or others in danger.
5. ***Learning.*** You need to be able to use efficient learning techniques to acquire and apply new knowledge and skills. And you need to know how to use your training, feedback, or other opportunities for self-learning and development.
6. ***Reading.*** You need to be able to understand, interpret, and learn from written material, including rules, regulations, instructions, and reports. And you need to be able to apply the knowledge you've gained from that written material to specific situations in the field.

PERSONAL CHARACTERISTICS

In addition to all of the above thinking skills, Border Patrol Agents are required to have certain personal characteristics, which the U.S. government contextually considers skills. These include the following six traits:

1. ***Conscientiousness.*** You need to display behavior that is dependable, organized, careful, and thoughtful, with great attention to detail and follow-through. You also need to display a high level of effort and commitment towards completing your work assignments.
2. ***Integrity and Honesty.*** You need to display high standards of ethical conduct, avoid even the appearance of impropriety, and be trustworthy in all work situations.
3. ***Emotional Maturity.*** You need to maintain self-control and approach potentially volatile situations, events, and people in a calm, professional manner.
4. ***Cooperativeness and Sensitivity to the Needs of Others.*** You need to collaborate effectively with others, you need to provide assistance—without hesitation—to people in need, you need to be sensitive to other cultures, and you need to have a genuine concern for others and their well-being.
5. ***Self-Presentation.*** You need to believe in your own self-worth, maintain an appropriate level of self-confidence, and display a professional image both on and off duty.
6. ***Flexibility.*** You need to be flexible. This means you must be open to change and new information. Also, you need to be able to adapt your behavior and work methods in response to new information, changing conditions, or unexpected obstacles. And they need to be able to deal effectively with ambiguity, because not all situations will be clear in terms of who or what is right or wrong.

INTERACTING WITH OTHERS

Six skills are required in this area of competency.

1. ***Writing.*** You need to use correct English grammar, punctuation, and spelling so that you can communicate facts, ideas, and messages in a succinct and organized manner. You also need to be able to write effectively and appropriately for your intended readers, who may be judges, U.S. attorneys, lawyers, and high-level politicians.
2. ***Oral Communication and Listening.*** You need to be able to express your ideas and facts to individuals or groups effectively, and you need to take into account the specific audience you're addressing and the nature of the information you're providing (because different audiences may require different approaches). In addition, you need to be able to speak clearly and articulate well. You need to be able to facilitate the open exchange of ideas. And you need to receive, attend to, interpret, and respond not only to verbal messages but also to other cues, such as body language.
3. ***Leadership.*** You need to be able to interact with others to influence, motivate, and challenge. You also need to set an example for others to follow, through you own personal conduct, professional appearance, and technical or administrative knowledge.
4. ***Teaching Others.*** You need to be able to help others to learn, and you need to identify others' training needs. You must provide constructive reinforcement (as opposed to negative feedback). You need to coach others so they can learn how to perform various tasks. And you need to be able to act as a mentor or source of information for others.
5. ***Negotiating.*** You need to work with others toward a mutually acceptable agreement that may involve exchanging specific resources or resolving differences. Therefore, you need to be able to build consensus through give-and-take.
6. ***Teamwork.*** You need to encourage and facilitate cooperation, pride, trust, and group identity. You also need to foster commitment and team spirit. In general, you need to be able to work with others to achieve your goals.

WORK MANAGEMENT SKILLS

The U.S. government has identified seven core skill sets that pertain to how well you manage your work.

1. ***Technology Application.*** You must be able to integrate technology—for example, computers—into the workplace, and you need to be able to use computers and computer applications to analyze data and communicate information. In addition, you need to be able to use technology in general to work more efficiently and to improve your work processes and products. There are courses available to help you with the most commonly used computer applications—specifically, Excel spreadsheets, Microsoft Word, Microsoft Outlook, and the Windows XP operating system.
2. ***Organizational and Community Awareness.*** This skill requires that you know how social, political, organizational, and technological systems work—and you need to be able to operate effectively within these systems. This also includes the policies, procedures, rules, and regulations not only of the specific agency you work for but also of the larger external environment in which you'll be working.
3. ***Managing and Organizing Information.*** You must be able to identify the need for information and then gather, organize, and maintain that information. You also need to be able to determine the importance and accuracy of the information, and be able to communicate it by a variety of methods.
4. ***Self-Management.*** You must be able to set well-defined and realistic personal goals for yourself, monitor your progress and be motivated to achieve, and manage your own time and deal with stress effectively.
5. ***Managing Resources.*** You need to be able to select, acquire, store, and distribute a variety of resources, including materials, equipment, and money. To do this effectively, you need to understand agency procurement regulations and budgeting and funding procedures.
6. ***Managing Human Resources.*** You must be able to plan, distribute, and monitor work assignments. You also need to ensure that employees are selected for and assigned to job tasks appropriately. You must

be able to perform personnel actions on subordinates and you need to be able to evaluate the work of employees and provide feedback on their performance.

7. ***Planning and Evaluating.*** You must be able to organize your work, set priorities, and determine what resources are required. You need to be able to determine your objectives and the strategies to achieve organizational goals. And you need to monitor and evaluate your progress against your goals.

PHYSICAL AND PSYCHOMOTOR SKILLS

Finally, the U.S. government requires Border Patrol Agents to have the following three physical and psychomotor skills.

1. ***Eye–Hand Coordination.*** You must be able to coordinate your eye movement with your fingers, wrists, or arms in order to move, carry, or manipulate objects or to perform other job-related tasks—such as using a firearm.
2. ***Physical Strength and Agility.*** You must be able to bend, lift, climb, and walk for long periods of time, and you must be able to perform physical work with ease.
3. ***Stamina.*** You must be able to perform repetitive or strenuous tasks for a long period of time.

The next two sections of this chapter provide more detailed information on the fitness requirements for being a Border Patrol Agent.

PRE-EMPLOYMENT FITNESS TESTING

The Border Patrol Agent position is a physically demanding law-enforcement position. Agents need to be able to perform strenuous duties under rigorous environmental conditions. For example, some physically challenging tasks of this occupation include

- pursuing and apprehending suspects
- walking and running long distances

- climbing and jumping
- moderate to heavy lifting
- swimming

These duties require physical stamina, upper- and lower-body endurance, and the ability to hold and operate various firearms for extended periods of time. Therefore, you must pass certain pre-employment fitness tests in order to be considered for a position as a Border Patrol Agent; you will take more fitness tests upon entering the Border Patrol Academy; and the Academy program includes further physical training programs considered to be among the most rigorous in the profession.

The pre-employment fitness test will be administered at the same time and location as your medical examination (which is described in detail in Chapter 4). The fitness test consists of three components, and you must pass all three tests; each test must be successfully completed before you can move on to the next test. Testing stops if you fail one of the three tests; moreover, failure on any one of the three tests means that you will not be hired for a Border Patrol Agent position, and no retesting is allowed. However, if you fail and subsequently improve your level of physical fitness, you can reapply for the Border Patrol Agent position under future vacancy announcements (in other words, you need to start your application process all over).

During the pre-employment fitness test, you will be required to do all of the following, in this sequence:

1. ***Perform 20 pushups in 60 seconds, using the proper form.*** The depth of the pushup will be measured by using a 4-inch-high foam block: your sternum (breastbone) must touch the foam block on each pushup. The test administrator will evaluate your form during the test and will count how many pushups you have done. If your pushups are not done in proper form, those pushups will not count, though you may continue to do pushups until the 60 seconds are over.
2. ***Perform 25 situps in 60 seconds, using the proper form.*** Your instructor will hold your feet during these situps. There should be an 18- to 24-inch separation from your heels and buttocks. Although situps done incorrectly don't count, you may continue to do situps until the 60 seconds are over.

3. ***Complete a 5-minute step test, stepping onto and off of a 12-inch bench, at a rate of 120–125 steps per minute.*** This is a cardiovascular endurance test.

Failure of any of these three tests stops the pre-employment fitness test. There will be a 3-minute rest period between each test. During this time, you will be shown how to perform the next exercise.

> For a detailed explanation of the proper form for each of these three tests, go to: http://www.cbp.gov/xp/cgov/careers/customs_careers/border_careers/fitness_requirements. This URL links to a 17-minute audio presentation that describes each test in detail and then gives you time to practice each test as it will actually be administered.

Additionally, you can find written details of the exercises, with pictures showing the proper form for each exercise, at the following website: http://www.cbp.gov/linkhandler/cgov/careers/customs_careers/border_careers/fitness_requirements/bp_agent_fit.ctt/bp_agent_fit.pdf.

Essentially, these three fitness tests measure your ability to move quickly with balance; your upper and lower body strength; and your aerobic capacity and endurance. If you are currently out of shape and not regularly exercising, you may want to consult your doctor or healthcare provider regarding a progressive exercise program that can help you prepare and get in shape for these tests. Your training regimen should include aerobic weight-bearing activities such as stepping, brisk walking, jogging, running, pushups, and situps.

Also, here are a few suggestions for the test day:

1. Avoid heavy physical exercise for 48 hours prior to test day.
2. Do not eat a large meal within two hours of testing.
3. Do not smoke or drink caffeine on the test day.
4. Practice is provided before the step test.

Successful completion of these three tests is really only the first step to being in shape: you must keep yourself in top physical condition from now on to ensure that you can successfully complete the rigorous requirements of the U.S. Border Patrol Academy and perform the duties of a Border Patrol Agent.

FITNESS TESTS AND TRAINING AT THE BORDER PATROL ACADEMY

If you pass all the required tests to become a Border Patrol Agent, you will then enter the Border Patrol Academy, where you will perform the following fitness tests:

1. Pushups: you need to do as many as you can in 60 seconds.
2. Situps: you need to do as many as you can in 60 seconds.
3. Pullups: you need to do as many as you can, though there is no time limit for pullups.
4. Running: you need to run 1.5 miles as fast as you can.

Finally, as mentioned, the 19-week course of training at the Academy also includes physical training and physical standards tests (discussed later in this chapter).

EDUCATION

You do not need any specialized education to become a Border Patrol Agent, but you do need to have either a bachelor's degree from an accredited four-year college, or some relevant work experience that exposed you to work in stressful situations where you had to make quick decisions—for example, in law enforcement or the military—or some combination of college education and relevant work experience. If you have (or if you are planning to get) your bachelor's degree, it can be in any major—anything from marketing to history, political science, business administration, accounting, economics, psychology—again, anything. Also, as described in Chapter 1, if you have at least one full year of graduate education in law or in a field related to law enforcement, such as criminal justice or police science, you may qualify to be hired at the GS-7 level.

If you don't have a college degree, and you're thinking long term and want to get your bachelor's degree before applying for a job as a Border Patrol Agent, you might consider getting a bachelor's degree in criminal justice. Fortunately, there are many institutions that offer accredited criminal justice degree programs. See Appendixes A and B for details.

THE CBP BORDER PATROL ACADEMY

If you're hired as a Border Patrol Agent, your first assignment will be to complete the 19-week training course at the Border Patrol Academy in Artesia, New Mexico, about 40 miles southwest of Roswell. This training center is on the site of the former Artesia Christian College, which the U.S. government purchased in June of 1989. It comprises 220 acres in the northwest section of the city of Artesia (population 14,000).

New recruits enter the Border Patrol Academy in groups of 50, and one or two groups enter each week. If you're hired and become part of one of these groups, you will attend classes eight hours a day on weekdays, and you will spend your weekends studying and preparing in other ways for the coming week.[2]

Training at the Border Patrol Academy is considered to be one of the most difficult in federal law enforcement, and you must maintain, on an ongoing basis, a passing score in *all* of the following courses of instruction in order to be retained:

- law courses
- Spanish-language training
- Border Patrol operations
- firearms training
- physical training
- driver training

The physical training at the Border Patrol Academy is *about equal* to Army basic training, according to one Border Patrol agent who was an Army veteran who then obtained his bachelor's degree in criminal justice. However, this agent also admitted that *it's a lot more academically challenging, not to mention that we all have to be proficient in Spanish when we graduate.*[3]

The next sections look at each of these courses in more detail.

Law Courses. The Border Patrol Academy law program consists of four separate courses.

1. Nationality Law: in this course, you will be taught how to determine the citizenship status of someone you are questioning, in order to discover whether that person is an alien, a U.S. citizen, or a U.S. national.
2. Immigration Law: in this course, you will be taught how to
   - ▷ verify the classification of aliens
   - ▷ determine the legality of status
   - ▷ recognize violations
   - ▷ initiate the appropriate action
3. Criminal Law: in this course, you will be taught how to recognize violations of federal criminal statutes and either take appropriate action (following the laws under the Department of Homeland Security's purview) or to refer the case to another federal agency of primary jurisdiction.
4. Statutory Authority: in this course, you will be taught the primary statutes, implementing regulations, and court decisions from which you, as a Border Patrol Agent, will derive your authority to act in various situations.

To complete this part of your training successfully, you need to attain, and continuously maintain, a minimum overall average of 70% in these four courses.

Spanish-Language Training. This part of your training consists of an 8-week task-based Spanish-language training program. More than one million undocumented aliens are apprehended by the U.S. Border Patrol each year, and 90% of them speak only Spanish, which is why it's critical for all Border Patrol Agents to speak Spanish. And if you want to be promoted, your proficiency in Spanish must increase until you are completely fluent.

The Spanish taught at the Border Patrol Academy is highly specific to the work you'll be doing and the type of conversations and interrogations you will need to have in order to do your job effectively. You will be taught law-enforcement language specific to your future work environment, and you will be taught how to solicit information from people. You will also be taught colloquial phrases and idiomatic expressions, so that you can talk naturally in Spanish.

Border Patrol Operations. This course consists of FLETC police training instruction, as well as an operations course instructed by Border Patrol personnel. FLETC stands for the Federal Law Enforcement Training Center, which is an interagency law-enforcement training organization that serves more than 80 federal agencies (obviously including the CBP). You will be tested midway through this training and then again at the end of the course. In order to successfully complete this aspect of your total training at the Academy, you must attain an overall grade of 70% in the combined subject areas.

Firearms Training. This part of your training includes both classroom and range practice shooting, to teach you what you need to know about the following topics:

- range safety
- survival shooting techniques
- judgment pistol shooting
- quick point
- instinctive reaction shooting (how to control your weapon in stressful situations to achieve maximum tactical accuracy and speed while quickly clearing any malfunction and to accomplish fast reloading; this skill builds confidence in your shooting ability under stress and instills an understanding of what your weapon can realistically do)

You'll have to wait until you get to the Academy for more information on these topics than you see here, because this is the only information provided in the CBP's brief description of what you'll learn at the Academy.

If you fail to complete your firearms training successfully, you will be provided eight hours of remedial training followed by a two-hour requalification session.

Physical Training. During your time at the Border Patrol Academy, you will also do physical fitness training two to three days per week initially, which will increase to five days per week after the midterm. This training consists of the following:

- 45–60 minutes of mat room work, including jumping jacks, pushups, situps, and strengthening exercises
- a 3-mile run at a 9–10-minute-per-mile pace.

The physical training program at the Academy has four purposes:

1. to condition you physically to an acceptable standard that will enable you to perform the day-to-day duties you will face as a Border Patrol Agent working in the field;
2. to train and condition you physically so that you can react well to obstacles (both from the environment and from people you may come in contact with) and so you can react well to physically dangerous situations (you need to be able to react in a way that minimizes injury to you or other agents or innocent third parties);
3. to condition you psychologically so that you are confident in your own physical ability, which in turn will enable you to react positively to physically strenuous or dangerous situations—and to ensure that you also know and remain aware of your physical limitations so that you are not overly confident in your physical abilities;
4. to teach you how important it is for you, as a Border Patrol Agent, to be physically fit and to maintain a fitness program that is right for you, after you leave the Academy.

The reason physical training is so important to Border Patrol work is that you will likely do much of your work on foot, often alone, and in rural areas: this is where the smuggling of illegal aliens, narcotics, and other contraband typically takes place, so you need to be in good shape, physically and psychologically, so that you can react and respond effectively in dangerous situations.

In order to graduate from the Border Patrol, you will be given a final, two-hour fitness test. You must be able to

- run 1.5 miles in 13 minutes or less
- run a 220-yard dash in 46 seconds or less
- complete the confidence course in two-and-a-half minutes or less

The brief description provided on the CBP's web site doesn't explain what the *confidence course* is, but the Marine Corps Basic Training includes a confidence course that consists of a combination of the following challenges:

- *The Confidence Climb:* here, you have to climb a vertical track (like a railroad track going up into the sky) about 30 feet to the top, straddle over the top log, and then descend on the other side.
- *The A-Frame*—here, you have to climb a rope and maneuver through three logs. Once you're through the logs, you walk approximately 20 feet over wooden beams to two A-shaped structures, then climb to the top, swing on a rope, and work your way slowly back down to the ground.
- *The Slide for Life*—here, you start by inching along a cable like a worm, over a swimming pool. Once you get across part of the cable, you need to hang by your hands, and face the end of the pool. Then, you need to kick up your legs to catch the cable and work your way to the end of the pool. Many people who attempt this lose their grip and fall into the pool.

Driver Training. This part of the Academy's program is intended to teach you how to operate a variety of vehicles safely and efficiently. Because the Border Patrol's main purpose is to prevent people from entering the United States illegally across our borders and to apprehend illegal aliens anywhere in the United States, Border Patrol Agents need to be able to operate vehicles under many different extreme conditions (both environmental and climate conditions).

To graduate from the Border Patrol Academy, you must successfully complete instruction in the following three areas:

1. van and utility vehicle operation
2. skid control
3. emergency response

Once you have completed the pass/fail portion of the driving program, you will then be given further advance instruction in these four areas:

1. pursuit driving
2. vehicle stops (both low-risk and high-risk)
3. night driving
4. four-wheel driving

POST-ACADEMY TRAINING

After you graduate from the Border Patrol Academy, you are still required to take Spanish and law and operations classes at the headquarters of the Border Patrol Sector to which you are assigned (the 20 sectors are listed in Chapter 1, in Exhibit 1-4, and shown on a map of the United States in Exhibit 1-5). You also need to pass two sets of probationary exams, seven and ten months after graduating. You will also receive on-the-job training as a member of a field-training unit led by at least one senior Agent. Mentoring by this senior Agent is critical: it is intended not only to help new Agents assimilate into the Agency but also to evaluate whether they have the aptitude and qualifications necessary for the rigorous demands of the job.[4]

POSSIBLE CHANGES TO TRAINING

After President Bush's decision to increase the number of Border Patrol Agents from about 12,000 to 18,000 by the end of 2008, the agency began considering ways to expedite its training process, in order to get new Agents out into the field faster. One approach it is considering is to cut 30 days from the schedule for trainees who already speak Spanish. Another is to convert post-academy classroom training to computer-based training, which would allow agents to complete their necessary once-a-week training at duty stations rather than traveling to sector headquarters (which is what new agents are currently required to do).

CHAPTER three

MILITARY ADVANTAGE AND PREFERENCE TO VETERANS

MILITARY VETERANS currently make up approximately 25% of the CBP's workforce.[1] The Border Patrol and other law-enforcement agencies are a good fit for military personnel who are leaving service. As one ex-military Senior Patrol Agent said, "it's an easier transition for [troops leaving the service] going from one uniform to the next. Adventure is there as well."[2] Another Border Patrol Agent, who spent $5\frac{1}{2}$ years in the Marine Corps, said that "the Border Patrol is not like the Corps [in that] there is not a strict chain of command, but a lot of situations are similar. The transition from the Corps to the Border Patrol was [therefore] pretty easy.[3]

The CBP recognizes the similarity of some aspects of the work, which is why it recruits from the military. As Randy Renn, a spokesman for the CBP, said, "Military veterans are used to working in all types of terrain and weather. Just like the Border Patrol, they are expected to be ready to deploy to any emergency at a moment's notice. It should be an easy transition from the military to the Border Patrol Agent career."[4]

One specific reason why it's a good idea to move from military to the Border Patrol is that you can apply your time served in the military to your federal retirement plan (although you have to buy back your time, either by making a lump-sum payment or by having small increments deducted from your Border Patrol paychecks). For example, the agent cited above applied his $13\frac{1}{2}$ years in the Marine Corps to his time with the Border Patrol, and when he retires with 20 years in the Border Patrol, he will receive retirement pay for $33\frac{1}{2}$ years of service.[5]

ELIGIBILITY FOR VETERANS' PREFERENCES IN HIRING

According to the Department of Labor,[6] veterans of the U.S. Armed Forces have been given some degree of preference in appointments to federal jobs—in fact, this has been true since the Civil War. Congress enacted laws to prevent veterans who are seeking federal employment from being penalized because of the time they spent in their military service, and to recognize that people who serve in the military make sacrifices that other people don't. Therefore, many veterans receive an advantage—in the form of a hiring preference determined by a point score—when they apply for federal jobs, including Border Patrol Agent jobs.

Here are the details on the laws that apply:

> By law (Title 5 USC, Section 2108), veterans who are disabled or who serve on active duty in the Armed Forces during certain specified time periods or in military campaigns are entitled to preference over non-veterans both in Federal hiring practices and in retention during reductions in force (RIF).
>
> The National Defense Authorization Act of 2006 (Public Law 109-163) extends Veterans' Preference to those individuals who served on active duty for a period of more than 180 consecutive days [i.e., 6 months] any part of which occurred during the period beginning on September 11, 2001, and ending on a future

date prescribed by Presidential proclamation or by law as the last date of Operation Iraqi Freedom; and, who were discharged or released from active duty in the armed forces under honorable conditions.

Note, however, that this doesn't mean these preferences will *ensure* that every veteran will be placed in every vacant federal job. In other words, you're not guaranteed a federal job just because you served in the military, because that practice would contradict the merit principle of public employment. What this *does* mean, though, is that *special consideration is given to qualified veterans seeking federal employment*—which includes the Border Patrol Agent job. However, it is critical for the applicant who is a veteran to understand that he or she must still otherwise be qualified for the position as a Border Patrol Agent, regardless of Veterans' Preference.

To determine if you are eligible for a veterans' preference, go to this website: www.dol.gov/elaws/vets/vetpref/mservice.htm. The site will ask you the following series of questions, at the end of which it will calculate how many points you may have toward your score, when you apply and are tested for nonmilitary law-enforcement jobs, such as the Border Patrol.

10-Point Preference in Hiring. You may be eligible for a 10-point preference in hiring if you can answer *yes* to all the following questions.

1. Did you serve on active duty in the Armed Forces of the United States?
2. Were you discharged from or released from active duty in the Armed Forces under honorable conditions?

   (If your discharge was Honorable or General, or was changed to Honorable or General by a Discharge Review Board, answer *yes*. If you received a clemency discharge, answer *no*.)
3. Do you have a present service-connected disability or receive service-connected compensation, disability retirement benefits or a pension from the military or the *Department of Veterans' Affairs*?

   (Note: *Service-connected disability* includes the award of a Purple Heart. Also, if you have applied for disability determination to the Department of Veterans' Affairs, and are likely to receive certification, answer *yes*. If you have not applied or do not have a pending determination of disability, answer *no*.)

If you answered *yes* to all of the above questions—in other words, if you served on active duty, received an honorable discharge, and are disabled because of your time on active duty—the site tells you that *you appear to be eligible for a 10-point preference in hiring.*

5-Point Preference in Hiring. On the other hand, if you answered *no* to Question 3, the site continues by asking you the following questions:

4. Did you retire from the military?
5. Did you serve during the period December 7, 1941, to July 1, 1955?
6. Did you serve for more than 180 consecutive days, any part of which occurred after January 31, 1955, and before October 15, 1976?
7. Did you serve on active duty during the period beginning August 2, 1990, and ending January 2, 1992?
8. Did you serve for more than 180 consecutive days, any part of which was served beginning on September 11, 2001, and ending on a date to be determined for Operation Iraqi Freedom?
9. Did you serve on active duty in the Armed Forces during a war, in a campaign or expedition for which a campaign medal was authorized, including Lebanon, Grenada, Panama, Southwest Asia (Desert Storm/Shield), Somalia, Haiti, the Persian Gulf and Bosnia?

If you answered *yes* to any one of Questions 4 to 9—i.e., if you did serve during active duty—the site provides this information: *You appear to be eligible for a 5-point preference in hiring.*

No Veterans' Preference in Hiring. If you answered no to Questions 4 to 9 (which basically are asking you whether or not you served during times of active duty, either in World War II, Korea, Vietnam, the first Gulf War, the Afghanistan and Iraq wars, and the other military campaigns mentioned in Question 9), the site then tells you that *you do not appear to be eligible for Veterans' Preference*. However, it does refer you to another source of information, to determine your possible eligibility under the *Uniformed Services Employment and Reemployment Rights Act (USERRA) of 1994.*

Here's another scenario, where the site asks you the following questions:

10. Did you retire from the military?
11. Are you drawing retirement pay from the military?
12. Did you retire at a rank of Major, Lieutenant Commander or higher?

If you answer *yes* to the above questions, the site informs you that *you do not appear to be eligible for Veterans' Preference.*

How the Eligibility Preference Points Help. If you are eligible for veterans' preference points, these points are added to your raw test score, *and* your test score is how the Border Patrol ranks you when they have positions open and are ready to make job offers. Obviously, a candidate with a score of 90 will be chosen and offered a job before someone with a score of 80, so if you have 5 or 10 points eligibility, that works to your advantage in being hired by the Border Patrol.

BORDER PATROL RECRUITING FROM THE MILITARY

The U.S. Border Patrol also actively recruits from the military. For example, in September of 2008, the agency participated in a *Recruit Military* job fair in Ashland, Nebraska. Approximately 30 other companies were also trying to recruit ex-military personnel, and approximately 200 military veterans attended the fair.[7] The Border Patrol is most interested in staff support and intelligence analysis jobs. A senior U.S. Border Patrol Agent based in Montana was the agency's representative at this fair, and he commented that "we are stepping up our recruiting, and recruiting in Nebraska is up 600% compared to previous years. We are recruiting like mad." And he explained why recruiting from the military makes sense: "when you get an opportunity to pull from the ranks of the military, you don't have to spend as much time on training. That is a huge plus."

In addition to recruiting here in the United States, the Border Patrol traveled overseas to recruit for the first time, in April of 2008. Two teams of agency officers visited six U.S. military bases in Germany, in hopes of recruiting military veterans when they leave their tours of duty overseas. And the trip was successful: the agents recruited 100 veterans to apply for positions as U.S. Border Patrol Agents.[8] The purpose of this trip was to address the need to fill President Bush's decision to add 6,000 more Border Patrol Agents by the end of 2008 (as discussed in Chapter 6). As in Nebraska, one of the recruiters who traveled to Germany confirmed why military veterans are so desired as potential Border Patrol Agents: "We are reaching out to the military because, like CBP, the military is committed to service to country and evokes the same professional attributes necessary for protecting the homeland."[9] Further, CPB recruiters attribute the success of former military personnel in jobs like Border Patrol Agent because they have comparable job experience, in terms of being self-disciplined; understanding, respecting, and following a chain of command; and working in the outdoors for long periods of time under varying—and often harsh—terrain and climate conditions.

As mentioned in the Introduction, the age limit for entry-level jobs in the Border Patrol was recently raised from age 37 to age 40. The primary reason for doing this was to enable more military veterans to apply for the job after they've completed a 20-year career in the military. For example, if you joined the Armed Forces when you were 18 years old and served the full 20 years, you were too old to apply for a job as a Border Patrol Agent when the age requirement was 37. With the age requirement changed to age 40, the Border Patrol can now benefit from your 20 years of military training and experience.

The Border Patrol has also worked with the National Guard at times. For example, in June of 2006, the National Guard began putting the first of a planned 2500 troops along the U.S.–Mexico border to work with the Border Patrol in curbing illegal immigration from Mexico. The National Guard already had about 450 personnel working along the border, fighting drug smuggling into the United States. But this additional assignment of National Guard personnel was implemented after President Bush announced that the Border Patrol would increase the number of agents from 12,000 to 18,000: until the new 6,000 agents could be recruited, tested, hired, and trained, the National Guard would help out as part of *Operation Jump Start*. The National Guard troops would not be involved in direct law enforcement activities; instead, they would provide direct support, helping detect possible illegal immigrants, and Border Patrol Agents would continue to apprehend and question people, as necessary.

The Department of Homeland Security is also considering offering incentives to current members of the reserves or former armed-service members who have two years of separation from service. The rationale behind this is that these personnel are already trained and physically fit, and many of the skills needed in military work and Border Patrol work are similar, though obviously the emphasis needs to shift from military to enforcement.

There are some critics, however, of this new approach to recruiting. For example, the Rev. Robin Hoover, founder of an organization called Humane Borders, feels this approach is akin to "militarizing the border." Hoover is concerned because soldiers are given so much weapons training that is not necessary for work as Border Patrol agents. Although Border Patrol Agents are trained in the use of firearms (as described in Chapter 2), critics like Hoover believe that agents "spend most of their time dealing with economic migrants who aren't dangerous,"[10] and "if [weapons training] is pre-eminent in your mind, you are going to be more apt to use [that training]."[11]

Nevertheless, the Border Patrol defends its practice of recruiting from the military as sensible. For example, Dave Stoddard, a former Border Patrol supervisor who retired in 1996 after 27 years with the agency, confirmed that nearly all of his classmates who graduated with him in 1969 from the Border Patrol academy were ex-military (Stoddard himself served three years in the Army before he joined the Border Patrol). And although that was 40 years ago, Stoddard feels the reasons for recruiting from the military are still solid today: "[The] military has rules of engagement [and the] Border Patrol has rules of engagement. . . . The former military guy knows how to take orders. He doesn't get panicked in emergency situations like coming under fire. He's already familiar with weapons and strategies and tactics. And, he has already dedicated three to six years to serving the country."[12] And T.J. Bonner, president of the National Border Patrol Council, which is the Border Patrol Agents' union, also believes that people with military experience who want to serve their country and have proved they can withstand rigorous training are a good match to work for the Border Patrol.[13]

CHAPTER four

THE APPLICATION PROCESS

TO APPLY to become a Border Patrol Agent, all you need to do is go to https://cbpmhc.hr-services.org/BPA/. This online application asks you questions about your background, qualifications, education, and experience. Also, as part of completing this application—that is, during the online application process—you will be asked to schedule when you will take the written test to qualify for the job. Also, as mentioned in the Introduction, the hardest part of the application process is the stringent background check.[1]

This chapter provides a preview of the questions you'll need to answer during this online application. Completing the online application takes about 30 minutes (depending on how quickly you can read and answer the questions).

BASIC PHYSICAL AND HEALTH REQUIREMENTS

The first question posed on the application is intended to make sure you know the physical and health requirements of the job. Chapter 2 described these in detail; in contrast, this section of the application is simply a paragraph summarizing the basic requirements.

- You must be physically able to perform strenuous duties under rigorous environmental conditions. These duties include
  - running long distances
  - climbing
  - jumping, etc.
  - withstanding exposure to extreme weather conditions for extended periods
  - standing and stooping for long periods of time
- You must be willing and able to work irregular and protracted hours.
- You must undergo a pre-employment medical exam and be medically certified to perform the full range of duties required, and to perform them efficiently and without hazard to yourself or to others.

This preliminary information describes some of the most common medical problems that prevent candidates from passing the medical exam, and describes the minimum standards necessary to avoid these problems.

- You must have uncorrected distance vision of 20/100 or better in each eye (which means that you can only see from 20 feet away what a person with normal vision can see from 100 feet away). Also, your binocular vision (i.e., seeing through both eyes) must be correctable to 20/20 vision with glasses or contact lenses.
- Your peripheral vision must be normal.
- Your visual depth perception must be normal.
- Your color vision must be normal (that is, you cannot be color-blind).
- Normal hearing is required, the use of any hearing aid to comply with the medical standards is unacceptable.

- Any disease or condition that interferes with the safe, efficient, and expected performance of your job duties or required training may constitute grounds for you to be disqualified for medical reasons.

The purpose of providing this preliminary information on the application is to ensure that candidates are not wasting their time by applying if they do not meet the basic medical standards required for the Border Patrol Agent job. Therefore, the first question after this information is *Do you wish to continue your application?*

In addition to the minimum standards listed above (which the online application will ask you about), there is more detailed information regarding medical diseases and conditions that may disqualify you from applying to become a Border Patrol Agent. These are available on the CBP's website,[2] and they include but are not limited to the following:

- **Vision.** Any disease or condition that interferes with your vision may be disqualifying. (Refractive surgical procedures, such as laser surgery and LASIK surgery, are considered acceptable provided your vision meets the CBP's vision standards post-operatively, and provided that an acceptable recovery time period has occurred and you are free of post-operative complications.)
- **Speech.** Any disease or condition that interferes with your speech or breathing or bears the potential to render you suddenly incapacitated is generally disqualifying.
- **Respiratory system.** Any disease or condition that interferes with respiratory function may be considered disqualifying. For example, asthma that is currently controlled on any medication is generally disqualifying.
- **Cardiovascular system.** Any disease or condition that interferes with cardiac function is generally disqualifying, for example, if you have a pacemaker or coronary artery disease.
- **Hypertension.** If your blood pressure is higher than 140 over 90, you may be disqualified.
- **Psychiatric disorders.** Any disorder that affects normal perceptual judgment and safe and acceptable behavior, or any evidence of

serious mental impairment, is generally disqualifying—for example, major depression, panic disorder, schizophrenia, or personality disorders.

- **Musculoskeletal system.** Any medical condition that interferes with or adversely impacts your movement, agility, flexibility, strength, dexterity, coordination, or the like is generally disqualifying, for example, arthritis, amputations (even of fingers), degenerative disk disease, fractures, or chronic low back pain.
- **Medications.** If you have taken narcotics, sedative hypnotics, barbiturates, amphetamines, or any other drug that has the potential for addiction for more than 10 days, you may be disqualified. This also pertains to anabolic steroids.
- **Endocrine and metabolic systems.** You may be disqualified if you have any excess or deficiency in hormonal production that can cause elevated blood pressure, weakness, fatigue, and/or collapse, such as insulin-dependent diabetes mellitus.
- **Gastrointestinal system.** You may be disqualified if you have any disorder that could incapacitate you or render you incapable of sustaining attention to required tasks—for example, if you have hepatitis or Crohn's disease.
- **Blood system.** You may be disqualified if you have anemia or hemophilia (or other blood diseases or conditions).

Again, for more detailed information on these and other diseases and conditions, go to the CBP's website. As mentioned, you will not be asked about these specific conditions during the online application, but this is something to keep in mind because you will be questioned about and possibly tested for these during your medical examination.

SUITABILITY FOR THE JOB

The next section of the online application is intended to ensure that a given applicant is suitable for the job itself and will meet the U.S. government's security standards. This section describes the intensive background investigation all applicants must undergo and indicates what the background investigation will be looking for—specifically:

- how honest you are
- how reliable you are
- if you have a police record
- what your financial records may reveal
- if you use alcohol or drugs
- your mental health
- your employment record

To obtain this information, the background investigation will include interviews with past and present employers, neighbors, teachers, friends, and references. The background investigation will also check law-enforcement records, credit records, educational records, medical records, and other records. Essentially, in this section, the CBP is giving you an opportunity to opt out of the application process if you think an investigation of your background will reveal something that would eliminate you from being considered for a Border Patrol Agent position. Therefore, after providing the above information, the application asks you, *Are you willing to undergo a background investigation for this position?*

Questions Regarding Use of Drugs. If you answer *yes* to the previous question and you continue the application process, the next section asks you the following more specific questions:

> Within the last 7 years, have you used, tried, experimented [with], purchased, sold, manufactured, or distributed a non-prescribed controlled substance (e.g., marijuana, anabolic steroids, ecstasy, oxycontin, rohypnol, GHB, ketamine, cocaine, methamphetamine, mushrooms, heroin, PCP, LSD, opium, hash)?

You can either answer *never* or specify during what time periods you did do any of the above (for example, within the past year).

Questions Regarding Citizenship and Immigration Status. Next, the application asks about your citizenship or immigration status in the United States, as well as that of your spouse and family.

After the age of 18, have you done any of the following:

- Did you enter the United States illegally?
- Did you overstay an authorized period of admission?
- Did you reside, work, or attend school in the United States without status?
- Did you violate or assist another to violate immigration or customs laws? Examples include:
  - smuggle an alien(s)
  - harbor/shelter an illegal alien
  - intentionally fail to declare merchandise or funds as required
  - make false claim to U.S. citizenship
  - attempt to enter the United States using fraudulent or counterfeit documents or documents belonging to another
- Were you ever removed or deported from the United States?
- Are you married to/living or residing with any person who is illegally in the United States (e.g., out of status, overstayed visa)?

Questions Regarding Conviction of Domestic Violence Crime. Your suitability for the job also involves the use of firearms, because all Border Patrol Agents are required to carry firearms. However, if you have ever been convicted of a misdemeanor crime of domestic violence, you will be disqualified from the Border Patrol Agent application process, because it is a felony for you to possess any firearms or ammunition. This section of the application defines and explains what constitutes a *misdemeanor crime of domestic violence.*

> A misdemeanor crime of domestic violence is generally defined as any offense which has, as an element, the use of attempted use or physical force or the threatened use of a deadly weapon, committed by a current or former partner, parent, or guardian of the victim. The term "convicted" excludes anyone whose conviction has been expunged or set aside, or who has received pardon.

The application then asks you, *Have you ever been convicted of a crime of domestic violence that has not been expunged or for which you have not received a pardon?*

Questions Regarding Your Finances. If you answer *no* to the previous questions and wish to continue with the online application, the next questions regarding your suitability for the job as a Border Patrol Agent pertain to your finances. Specifically, the application asks you:

> Are you currently delinquent on Federal Debt for 90 days or more (e.g., taxes, overpayment of benefits, federal guaranteed or insured loans, such as student and home mortgage loans)?

Questions Regarding U.S. Residency. One of the requirements of the Border Patrol Agent job is that you must be a U.S. citizen and you must have resided in the United States for the three years prior to when you apply for the position. This section of the online application provides details on this requirement, noting that you must have met one of the following conditions:

(a) [you must have] physically resided in the United States or its protectorates or territories (Guam, Puerto Rico, Virgin Islands, etc.), excluding short trips abroad (such as vacations);

OR

(b) [you must have] worked for the U.S. government as an employee overseas in a Federal or military capacity;

OR

(c) [you must have] been a dependent of a U.S. Federal or military employee serving overseas.

The online application goes on to say that exceptions may be granted to applicants if they can provide information explaining (to the U.S. government's satisfaction, of course), why they were living outside the United

States during the three years before applying for the Border Patrol Agent position. This information will be used to determine whether an applicant meets suitability and security requirements. The online application calls this information *state-side coverage information* and offers the following examples:

1. If you were working in another country for a U.S.-based company, you must provide the U.S. address of the company headquarters where your personnel file is located;
2. If you were a student at a U.S. college or university and you were studying abroad, you must provide the state-side address of the professor who was in charge of your study-abroad program;
3. If you were a member of a U.S.-based religious organization and you were doing religious work for that organization in another country, you must provide records from that religious organization for the mission work you were doing;
4. If you were working or studying overseas, you must also provide the U.S. addresses of anyone you worked with or studied with while you were overseas.

The online application then asks you to state whether or not you meet the CBP's U.S. residency requirements.

LANGUAGE ABILITY REQUIREMENTS

The next section of the online application pertains to the requirement that all Border Patrol Agents must speak or learn Spanish at the Border Patrol Academy. Here you must indicate your willingness to take a written test to determine your Spanish-language skills or to take an artificial language exam, which evaluates your ability to learn a foreign language. You must also state that you are willing to attend the required Spanish-language training course at the Border Patrol Academy.

DEBARMENT: IF YOU'VE BEEN BANNED FROM EMPLOYMENT

The next section of the online application states that applicants can be banned from employment for a specific time period if they are found unsuitable. It then asks you if you are currently debarred from entry-level officer positions, based on a decision made by any of the following organizations:

- the Office of Personnel Management
- the former Immigration and Naturalization Service
- the former Customs Service
- the Department of Homeland Security
- U.S. Customs and Border Protection

SETTLEMENT AGREEMENTS THAT RESTRICT THE APPLICATION PROCESS

The next section of the online application refers very briefly to settlement agreements. It states and asks only the following:

> An individual who currently applies for a Federal Career Intern Program (FCIP) position and is found unsuitable for employment has certain appeal rights to the Merit Systems Protection Board.
>
> Are you under a settlement agreement which currently restricts you from applying for or being considered for employment in a Border Patrol Agent position?

Again, the intent of such questions is to let applicants know of possible impediments to their application for a Border Patrol Agent position.

ABILITY TO PERFORM ESSENTIAL FUNCTIONS OF A BORDER PATROL AGENT

New recruits for the position of Border Patrol Agent, of course, receive extensive training at the Border Patrol Academy before they begin any official job duties. However, the CBP uses this next section of the online application to ask 12 key questions regarding your ability to perform some of the essential functions of the Border Patrol Agent job. This section of the application is critical, because it explicitly states that *if you answer* no *to one or more of the following Essential Function questions, you may be disqualified from further consideration for the Border Patrol Agent position.*

Here are the questions, to which you simply answer *yes* or *no*:

1. Applicants are required to undergo a drug screening and will be subject to random drug testing after employment. Will you comply with this requirement?
2. Applicants are required to undergo a comprehensive medical examination. Will you comply with this requirement?
3. Border Patrol Agents encounter people (aliens) experiencing extreme poverty and personal hardship, such as separation from family. Agents may also witness drownings, vehicle accidents and other tragedies. Agents are occasionally exposed to aliens who carry infectious diseases. Would you be able to work in these conditions?
4. Would you be able to work alone in remote areas throughout the night or at times when you may have limited communication or may be at a high risk of danger?
5. Proficiency in the Spanish language is required for effective performance in the Border Patrol Agent job. Would you be willing to learn the language at the required level of proficiency?
6. New Border Patrol Agents are required to attend a rigorous five-month (20-week) training program. Would you be willing to attend such training in a location that may be away from your current residence?
7. Some new Border Patrol Agents will be assigned to small, remote locations or areas in which there are people whose cultures are significantly different from their own. If assigned to such an area, would you be willing to relocate?

8. Border Patrol Agents are assigned initially to the Southwest border, after which transfers to all future duty stations, as well as promotions, are made on a competitive basis. Would you be willing to work at a duty station away from your original home for an indefinite period of time?
9. On occasion, Border Patrol Agents are assigned on very short notice to work on a temporary basis, but for an extended period of time, in locations away from their permanent duty station. Would you be willing to accept such assignments?
10. Would you be able to work a schedule that could include changing your days off within the seven calendar days of Sunday through Saturday?
11. The Border Patrol requires mandatory use of a prescribed uniform and conformity to established grooming standards. Would you be willing to comply with these requirements?
12. If you found yourself in a "life threatening" situation, do you feel you could use deadly force (e.g., use your firearm) to protect your life, the lives of fellow officers, or the lives of innocent bystanders?

SCHEDULING YOUR ORAL INTERVIEW

The next section of the online application covers scheduling for a structured oral board interview, which will be conducted for all applicants who successfully complete the written test and who are tentatively selected for a position. Therefore, you must now choose a location where you wish to take the structured oral interview. The online application says there are 47 possible locations to choose from, but there are actually 49, in 30 states and Puerto Rico.

Some of the larger states have more than one city listed: for example, Arizona has two cities, California has two, Florida has three, New York has five, Texas has ten, and Washington State has two. Exhibit 4-1 lists the cities and states from which you can choose, listed in alphabetical order by state first.

EXHIBIT 4-1. Cities and States Where Oral Board Interviews Are Held

1. Alabama, Mobile
2. Arizona, Tucson
3. Arizona, Yuma
4. Arkansas, North Little Rock
5. California, San Diego
6. California, Stockton
7. Colorado, Denver
8. Florida, Jacksonville
9. Florida, Orlando
10. Florida, Pembroke Pines
11. Georgia, Atlanta
12. Idaho, Twin Falls
13. Illinois, Chicago
14. Indiana, Indianapolis
15. Louisiana, Baton Rouge
16. Maine, Houlton
17. Massachusetts, Boston
18. Michigan, Detroit
19. Minnesota, Fort Snelling (St. Paul)
20. Montana, Great Falls
21. Nevada, Las Vegas
22. New Mexico, Artesia
23. New York, Albany
24. New York, Buffalo
25. New York, Champlain
26. New York, New York City
27. New York, Tonawanda
28. North Carolina, Charlotte
29. North Dakota, Grand Forks
30. Ohio, Cleveland
31. Oregon, Portland
32. Pennsylvania, York
33. Puerto Rico, Ramey
34. Tennessee, Nashville
35. Texas, Dallas
36. Texas, Del Rio
37. Texas, El Paso
38. Texas, Harlingen
39. Texas, Houston
40. Texas, Laredo
41. Texas, Lubbock
42. Texas, Marfa
43. Texas, McAllen
44. Texas, San Antonio
45. Utah, Salt Lake City
46. Vermont, Swanton
47. Virginia, Fairfax
48. Washington, Seattle
49. Washington, Spokane

Note that there are *no* locations in the following states and districts:

1. Alaska
2. Connecticut
3. Delaware
4. Hawaii
5. Iowa
6. Kansas
7. Kentucky
8. Maryland
9. Mississippi
10. Missouri
11. Nebraska
12. New Hampshire
13. New Jersey
14. Oklahoma
15. Rhode Island
16. South Carolina
17. South Dakota
18. Washington DC
19. West Virginia
20. Wisconsin
21. Wyoming

WILLINGNESS TO ACCEPT PLACEMENT IN SPECIFIC GEOGRAPHIC LOCATIONS

After you've chosen the site at which you would like to be interviewed, the online application next informs you of the geographic locations where you are most likely to be assigned, if you pass all tests and become a Border Patrol Agent. This information is very clear:

> Applicants must be willing to accept placement anywhere along the Southwest border of the United States. However, you will be able to identify the one location where you would prefer to

work. . . . Please choose one geographic location where you would be willing to work:

- ***South Texas*** (includes the Laredo Border Patrol Sector and the Rio Grande Valley Border Patrol Sector)
- ***West Texas/New Mexico*** (includes the Del Rio Border Patrol Sector, El Paso Border Patrol Sector, and Marfa Border Patrol Sector)
- ***California*** (includes the El Centro Border Patrol Sector and San Diego Border Patrol Sector)
- ***Arizona*** (includes the Tucson Border Patrol Sector and Yuma Border Patrol Sector).

Chapter 1 provided a map of the 20 Border Patrol Sectors; Exhibit 4-2 shows it again, for easy reference.

Also, keep in mind that while you may turn down appointment to a particular location, this is not advisable, as you may not receive another offer.

EXHIBIT 4-2. Map of the 20 Sectors Comprising the Office of Border Patrol

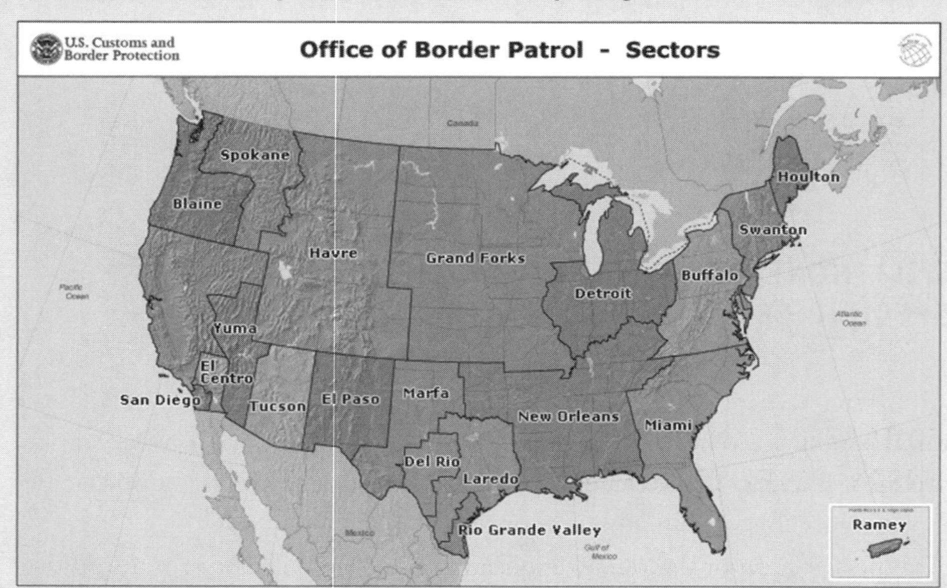

From www.cbp.gov/linkhandler/cgov/careers/customs_careers/border_careers/bp_agents/sectors_map.ctt/Sectors_map.pdf.

BIOGRAPHICAL INFORMATION

Up until this point in the online application, all of the questions you've been asked have been anonymous—in other words, you haven't yet provided any identifying information about yourself, so if you opted out at any time, the CBP has no record that you ever even began the online application process. And that was the purpose of those questions: to enable you to think about what might disqualify you from consideration for employment (such as prior drug use or criminal convictions), or what might make you rethink your decision to pursue such employment (such as an unwillingness to work in certain locations in the United States).

If you're still on board, this point in the application process asks you to provide all of the following information:

- your social security number
- your date of birth
- your first name, middle initial, and last name
- your street address and the city, state, zip code, and country where you currently reside
- at least one home phone number (and you can enter up to two alternate phone numbers)
- the best time to reach you by phone (day, night, or either)
- your mother's maiden name

Most of these fields are required; if you leave them blank, you will not be able to move forward with your online application.

EDUCATION AND EXPERIENCE FOR ENTRY-LEVEL BORDER PATROL AGENTS

The next section of the online application asks you questions regarding your education and experience, so that the CBP can determine what grade level you are eligible for. You will be considered at the highest grade level for which you are qualified. The online application is simply making a preliminary eligibility determination, which will be verified later in your application, interview, and testing process.

As mentioned in Chapter 1 in the salary section, there are three grade levels at which you can be hired, depending on your education and experience: GS-5, GS-7, and GS-9.

GS-5 Level. You may qualify for this level of employment through work experience, education, or a combination of work experience and education. *A bachelor's degree is not required for this level*; however, the application asks you here whether or not you have a bachelor's degree or a higher degree from an accredited college or university.

GS-7 Level. You may qualify for this level of employment based on any of the following:

- graduate-level education: one or more complete years of full-time graduate-level study (after you received your bachelor's degree); note that the graduate-level education must be in police science, law, or a field related to law enforcement
- superior academic achievement: this is based on your receiving a bachelor's degree, such as a B.S or B.A., and any of the following required achievements:
  - class standing: you must be in the upper third of your graduating class in your college, university, or major subdivision
  - (or) grade-point average: 3.0 or higher for all completed undergraduate courses, or courses complete in the last two years of undergraduate study; or a GPA of 3.5 or higher for all courses in your major field of study, or required courses in major complete in the last two years of undergraduate study
  - (or) honor society membership: you must have been a member of a national scholastic honor society other than freshman honor societies
- specialized experience
- (or) a combination of specialized experience and graduate-level education

GS-9 Level. You may qualify for this level of employment if you have one year of specialized experience in law enforcement or other responsible work that would therefore be equivalent to the GS-7 level and that would demonstrate your ability to do all of the following:

- Develop cases, conduct interviews or interrogations, apprehensions, and arrests in order to further the process or case development.
- Prepare cases and appear as a professional witness in court.
- Exercise sound judgment in the use of firearms and conduct training, qualification exercises, or courses in the proper care and use of firearms.
- Deal effectively with individuals or groups of persons in a courteous and tactful manner in their detention, control, or interrogation, and work to promote effective community outreach programs and public relations.
- Analyze and disseminate intelligence information and data rapidly; and apply a practical knowledge of the laws, concepts, operational practices and law enforcement methods and techniques in order to independently perform duties typically encountered in law enforcement.
- Develop and maintain contact with a network of informants, social and political organizations, state and local enforcement agencies, and private citizens, to ensure continuity of enforcement work and to carry out enforcement responsibilities.
- Use a variety of law enforcement databases and information retrieval systems, such as NEXUS as well as:
  - TECS, the Treasury Enforcement Communication System, which is a computerized information system designed to identify individuals and businesses suspected of or involved in violation of federal law. TECS is also a communications system permitting message transmittal between Treasury law enforcement offices and other national, state, and local law enforcement agencies. [3]
  - NCIC, the National Crime Information Center, which is a computerized index of criminal justice information (pertaining to criminal record history information, fugitives, stolen property, and missing persons) that is available to Federal, state, and local law

enforcement and other criminal justice agencies and is operational 24 hours a day, 365 days a year. This information assists authorized agencies in criminal justice and related law enforcement objectives, such as apprehending fugitives, locating missing persons, locating and returning stolen property, as well as in the protection of the law enforcement officers encountering the individuals described in the system. [4]

- Prepare reports and write other documents that deal with the collection, protection, and recording of evidence, the presentation of testimony, and the retention of informational materials concerning illegal activities and practices encountered during daily activities.

After listing what you need to be able to do in order to qualify for the GS-9 level of employment as a Border Patrol Agent, the online application then asks you to answer *yes* or *no* to eight questions that essentially ask if you can do all of the above just listed. The application emphatically states that Your experience must demonstrate that you have the *ability to meet all eight (8) of the following elements.*

Once you answer these questions, the online application asks you to select the grades for which you wish to be considered.

VETERAN STATUS

Next, the online application asks whether you are a veteran of the U.S. Armed Forces, and if you were discharged under honorable conditions. (Recall that Chapter 3 provided information regarding military experience.)

SCHEDULING AND TAKING THE WRITTEN EXAM

The next sections of the online application provide information on the written test you will be required to take as part of your application process. Keep in mind, as noted in Chapter 1, that only about 40% of people who apply to become Border Patrol agents actually pass the written exam because it is so difficult. Therefore, the Border Patrol strongly advises applicants to study rigorously for the test by using the study guides that the agency provides free to applicants. You should also consider using other study guides and practice tests, such as those provided by Learning Express: see our *Border Patrol Exam: The Complete Preparation Guide*, which also includes access to a free online practice test that also gives you instant scoring.

Back to this part of the online application process, you will be informed that the CBP agency provides reasonable accommodation in terms of special testing arrangements for applicants with disabilities, where appropriate. These accommodations may include changes in the presentation format, response format, assessment setting, timing, or scheduling, and determinations of requests for reasonable accommodation will be made on a case-by-case basis. No further information is provided regarding what type of disabilities might be accommodated. In contrast, this section simply asks whether you have a physical disability or any other type of impairment that would require special testing arrangements at the test site in order for you take the written test. This section concludes with a note stating that if you answer *yes* regarding your need for special testing arrangements, someone from an OPM will contact you to discuss your request.

Next, information is provided on the locations at which you can take the written test, which include all 50 states as well as the District of Columbia, Guam, Puerto Rico, and the Virgin Islands.

In addition, the CBP has a limited number of sites where compressed testing is conducted. At a compressed test session, your test results—whether you pass or fail—are provided shortly after you complete the exam. In addition, you also receive an orientation and can discuss a career with a Border Patrol recruiter. Finally, applicants who pass the test receive a tentative selection package at the test site, including an oral interview appointment date, pre-employment forms, and other hiring process information. As you can see, the advantage of compressed testing is that it significantly reduces the time involved in the pre-employment process. You need to travel at your own expense to these sites. And you should be prepared to spend approximately eight hours at the test site.

Compressed testing is offered only at the locations listed in Exhibit 4-3 (subject to change, but this information should be accurate when you complete your own online application); these are listed alphabetically here by state first.

Exhibit 4-3. Compressed Testing Locations for the Written Exam

1. Arizona: Phoenix and Tucson
2. California: Holtville, Moreno Valley, Ontario, and San Diego
3. Colorado: Denver
4. Florida: Orlando
5. Georgia: Atlanta
6. Illinois: Chicago
7. Michigan: Detroit
8. New York: Buffalo and New York City
9. Pennsylvania: Philadelphia
10. Puerto Rico: San Juan
11. Texas: Dallas, El Paso, Houston, McAllen, Pharr (in the Rio Grande Valley), and San Antonio
12. Washington: Bellevue

Once you choose the location where you want to take the written test, the application will offer you a choice of three available test sessions, which may be three to eight weeks from the date you are completing your online application. To continue with your application, you must choose one of these dates and set up a time to take the written test. However, the last question you will be asked is whether or not you want to submit the application you just filled out, so if you're not yet sure you want to apply, you can opt out. Keep in mind, though, that you can't save your application, so if you decide to come back another day to apply online, you'll have to start all over again. Fortunately, as mentioned, it takes only about 30 minutes to answer all questions.

Chapter 5 describes the written test and provides suggestions on how to prepare for taking it.

CHAPTER five

PREPARING FOR THE U.S. BORDER PATROL AGENT EXAM

AS MENTIONED in Chapter 4, you will register to take the Border Patrol written exam as part of completing your online application. The application will give you three future dates on which you can take the exam in the location you specify, and once you choose one of those dates, you will be registered to take the test. This chapter describes what the exam covers, and it provides information on how to prepare for the written exam.

OVERVIEW OF THE U.S. BORDER PATROL EXAM

The U.S. Border Patrol Exam is a written exam that consists of three tests, although you will take only two of them:

1. a Logical Reasoning Test
2. a Spanish Language Proficiency Test
3. an Artificial Language Test (ALT)

All applicants take the Logical Reasoning Test and either the Spanish Language Proficiency Test or the ALT.

This chapter describes each of these tests in detail, so you'll know generally what to expect, including sample questions, with the correct answers, and explanations of the answers. This chapter also provides information on practice tests and other resources that can help you further when you take the written test. You can download a *Preparation Manual for the U.S. Border Patrol Test* at the following website: www.tsa.gov/assets/pdf/soar/preparation_manual_bpa.pdf.

The Border Patrol strongly recommends that anyone planning to apply to become a Border Patrol Agent download this test and become familiar with the types of questions on the test. In other words, *don't take the test without any preparation*. This *Preparation Manual* explains each of the three tests in detail. It also offers some test-taking tips that can help you, especially if you haven't had much practice taking written, multiple-choice tests (such as the SAT, or Standard Aptitude Test, which high-school students take before applying to college). Exhibit 5-1 offers a summary of the test-taking tips.

LearningExpress offers another book, *The Border Patrol Exam: The Complete Preparation Guide*, which covers the three tests in more detail than we can here in Chapter 5; it includes

- two complete practice test based on the official Border Patrol Exam
- free access to an online Border Patrol practice exam, to help you identify and correct any weak areas you may have so you can devote extra study time to those areas
- a free online diagnostic report—that is, an instant score—that will show you exactly where you need to study more

EXHIBIT 5-1. Tips for Taking the U.S. Border Patrol Exam

1. Stay calm and relaxed when taking the test. Breathe slowly and deeply, to help you stay calm.
2. Read the directions very carefully before you being to take the test.
3. Begin by answering the questions you find easiest to answer. Skip questions that you find to be difficult; then come back to them later. But be careful: if you skip a question, make sure you find the correct place to answer the next question—in other words, make sure your answers correspond to the right questions.
4. Read each question completely, and then read all answer choices carefully before you select and mark your answer on the answer sheet. If you do not know the answer to a particular question, try to eliminate some of the answer choices: if you know that some choices are incorrect—or even probably incorrect—you have a better chance of choosing the correct answer by guessing from the remaining choices.
5. Answer every question, even if you have to guess. Keep in mind that your score is based *only* on the number of questions you answer correctly. In other words, you are not penalized for answering questions incorrectly, which is why you should *guess* an answer even if you don't *know* the answer.
6. If you finish the test before your time is up, go back and check your answers.
7. Be sure to mark your answer sheet correctly. If you have to change an answer, erase your first answer before you mark your new answer. And, as mentioned in tip 3, if you skip a question, be sure to answer the next question in the appropriate place on your answer sheet. It would be a shame to know all the correct answers to all questions, but then mark them in the wrong places.
8. If you happen to notice a pattern of responses on your answer sheet (for example, *A* followed by *B*, then *C*, then *D*, then *E*, or a pattern of three As followed by two Bs—or any other pattern), ignore it! There is no way to improve your chances on the test by guessing based on some answer sheet pattern. The correct answers are chosen randomly, so any pattern is just a coincidence.
9. If you are proficient in standard Spanish, including grammar (which is heavily tested), take the Spanish Language Proficiency Test. If you are not proficient in Spanish, take the ALT.

Both the Learning Express book and the U.S. Border Patrol's official *Preparation Manual* are especially useful because they provide *explanations* for why the correct answer choice is correct as well as why the other choices are incorrect. These explanations should help you enormously when you are studying to take the written exam.

THE LOGICAL REASONING TEST

There are 30 questions on this part of the exam. The questions are multiple choice (and you have five possible responses from which to choose). The questions assess several key intellectual capabilities that are required for you to succeed as a Border Patrol Agent—specifically

- your knowledge of vocabulary—including legal terms (which are often Latin-language terms, such as *ex post facto* (These Latin terms are usually defined on the test, but of course they won't be when you're working on the job. Exhibit 5-2 provides a list of some of the terms you may encounter.)
- your reading comprehension—because you need to be able to read documents and reports and understand what you've read and the implications of that information to the case you're working on and the people involved
- critical thinking skills—because the Border Patrol Agent position is not simply to guard borders but to be able to assess potentially

EXHIBIT 5-2. A Sampling of Latin Terms that May Appear on the Exam

causa mortis	a transaction between a person who expects to die soon and another living person—usually used in the context of giving a gift; contrast with *inter vivos*
dolus bonus	permissible deceitfulness
dolus malus	unlawful deceitfulness
ex post facto	(laws) enforced retroactively
inter vivos	a transaction between a living person and another living person—usually used in the context of giving a gift; contrast with *causa mortis*
jus soli	citizenship determined by the place of one's birth
jus sanguinis	citizenship determined by descent (i.e., by one's parents or other relative)

dangerous situations (and people) and determine how best to handle those situations

All of the above skills are necessary because Border Patrol Agents are often required to testify in court and other legal proceedings, so you need to understand the legal reasoning process. The questions on the Logical Reasoning part of the Border Patrol Exam will test your ability to do exactly that. Finally, keep in mind that, fortunately, the questions test *only* your understanding of the facts presented in each questions, and you do *not* need to know any other information beyond what is presented to you. The questions simply test your ability to understand the information you read and to draw a logical conclusion from those facts.

The Logical Reasoning questions may cover such topics as

- determining whether or not someone is a legal U.S. citizen, based on different laws passed at different times and specific family circumstances
- determining whether or not someone can be deported, based on different laws passed at different times
- determining whether or not someone who wishes to enter (or who has entered) the United States is entitled to refugee status or asylum status
- assessing how the statute of limitations applies in prosecuting different crimes, depending on whether they are felonies, misdemeanors, or petty misdemeanors (all of which will be defined in the question)
- evaluating how different legal philosophies would apply in different cases—for example, under what circumstances someone might be tried for murder or under what circumstances the death penalty might apply, if different judges with different philosophies were presiding over the same murder case
- assessing valid reasons, based on provided regulations and laws, for someone to apply for refugee status from his or her home country

- evaluating what involvement in a particular crime constitutes *conspiracy* (again, as with all questions on the exam, your answer will depend on the facts presented to you within the question)
- interpreting whether people's basic human rights also carry responsibilities, according to information included in the *Universal Declaration of Human Rights*
- understanding the implications of such laws as the Immigration and Nationality Act (INA) and how they might apply, for example, to whether or not it is unlawful for someone who has been transporting one or more illegal aliens
- understanding what statements made by a criminal defendant are admissible in court and which are not
- understanding what constitutes *deadly force*
- recognizing which crimes are more serious than others (for example, theft or prostitution?)
- evaluating when a person's property can be seized by creditors and when it cannot be
- understanding how federal laws and state laws on immigration may conflict, and assessing the implications of those conflicts
- understanding the difference between real property and personal property
- understanding the implications of reported statistics—for example, pertaining to crime rates—in order to assess validity
- making connections, or recognizing that there is no connection, between different statistics—for example, the number of people who are *inspected* at a particular border and the number of people who were *apprehended* at the same border

These questions are not easy. Exhibit 5-3 shows a few examples from a practice test. As mentioned at the beginning of this chapter, the Border Patrol *strongly recommends* that you download the free *Preparation Manual*, to familiarize yourself with and practice answering the logical reasoning questions on the test.

Exhibit 5-3. Sample Questions from the Logical Reasoning Test

1. Citizenship for foreign-born children is defined by guidelines that have been revised during past decades. Between 1952 and 1986, citizenship was granted when one parent was a United States citizen and one an alien, providing the citizen parent had been physically present in the United States for ten years, at least five of which were after attaining the age of 14. After 1986, the guidelines changed. Citizenship was approved when one parent was a citizen and one an alien, but the citizen parent had to have been physically present in the United States for five years, at least two of which were after attaining the age of 14. Baby Jon was born in the year 1995 to Chimera Ballard (an alien) and Roger Ballard (a U.S. citizen). Jon is NOT considered a citizen from birth.

If the above information is true, then it can be validly concluded that the most likely true statement regarding Jon's parents is that, at the time of Jon's birth

a. Roger and Chimera were both 25 years old; Chimera had been present in the United States since 1984 and Roger since 1994.
b. Roger was 25 years old and had been present in the United States since 1994.
c. Roger was 15 years old and had been present in the United States since 1993.
d. Roger and Chimera were both 17 and had been present in the United States between 1991 and 1992.
e. Roger was 16 years old and had been present in the United States since 1993.

8. A person arrested for a felony has a right to representation by an attorney and has certain rights against self-incrimination. If a defendant in a criminal trial chooses not to testify in a criminal trial, neither the judge nor prosecution may comment adversely on his/her decision. In addition, the defendant in a criminal trial has the right to have the judge instruct the jury not to draw any adverse inference from the defendant's failure to testify. If a defendant accused of a criminal act refused to comment during a custodial police interrogation, neither the prosecutor nor the judge may comment on this fact at the later criminal trial. If the defendant accused of a criminal act was silent *before* being arrested, this fact *may* be commented on at the later criminal trial. In a civil trial, either side may comment on a defendant's decision not to testify.

From the information given above, it CANNOT be validly concluded that

a. If the defendant pleads self-defense to a murder charge but did not report the killing until two weeks after it occurred, this fact can be commented on at trial.
b. If the defendant pleads not guilty to a murder charge and refuses to talk to police after being arrested, this fact cannot be commented on at trial.
c. If the defendant pleads not guilty at a civil trial for wrongful death and decides not to testify in her own defense, this fact can be commented on.
d. If the defendant pleads not guilty at a civil trial in which he is being sued because of aggravated assault, a judge may compel him to testify.
e. If the defendant is accused of murder but refuses to talk to police after being arrested, this fact cannot be commented on at trial.

(Continued)

EXHIBIT 5-3. Continued

23. States may not usurp the federal power over immigration. The Supreme Court overturned an Arizona statute restricting alien employment because the statute ran contrary to the implied intent of Congress that aliens who are permitted to enter the country under federal immigration law be allowed to earn a living. Similarly, the Court rejected state laws setting residency requirements for aliens seeking welfare. The fact that federal legislation takes precedence over every other type can, however, work against aliens, as well. Federal courts have rejected an assertion that the immigration quota system is inconsistent with the U.N. Charter. Moreover, aliens who have been excluded from immigrating have no constitutional right to a hearing.

From the information given above, it can be validly concluded that the U.N. Charter

a. prohibits excluded aliens from having a hearing.
b. favors quotas for allowing aliens into the United States.
c. does not favor quotas for allowing aliens into the United States.
d. has many similarities to the U.S. Constitution.
e. supports residency requirements for aliens to receive welfare.

27. Assume the following statistics are true: A *New York Times* story reports that this year, crimes by people under 18 have risen 47% over last year. *U.S.A. Today* reports that this year, the number of homicides committed by children under 12 has grown 125% since last year. Yet, Justice Department statistics show that fewer than 40 children under the age of 13 (out of all such children in the United States) were convicted of murder this year. 4% of newspapers and TV programs are about children. Of those, 40% are concerned with children in connection with crime and violence.

From the information given above, it can be validly concluded that, by the way they report statistics

a. the news media gives an inaccurate picture of the actual number of children involved in violent crimes.
b. the news media always downplays the numbers of children who are involved in violent crimes.
c. the news media tends to give an accurate picture of the involvement of children in violent crimes.
d. the news media has proven that children in general are less violent now than they were 20 years ago.
e. the news media has proven that children in general are more violent now than they were 20 years ago.

THE SPANISH-LANGUAGE PROFICIENCY TEST

As reiterated throughout this book, all Border Patrol Agents are required to know the Spanish language. Therefore, all applicants are required to take *either* the Spanish-Language Proficiency Test *or* the ALT. If you already know Spanish—including grammar and vocabulary, not just colloquial Spanish—you should obviously take the Spanish-Language Proficiency Test. If you do not have a strong command of Spanish, you should take the ALT.

The sample questions provided in the CBP's *Preparation Manual for the U.S. Border Patrol Test* will help you become familiar with both the type of questions asked and the level of difficulty of the questions on the test. (These can also help you decide which test you should take, if you're not sure of your knowledge of Spanish.) However, keep in mind that these questions cannot *teach* you Spanish—or even enough Spanish so that you can pass the Border Patrol's test; that is not what the sample questions are intended to do. They are only intended to familiarize you with the type of questions you will be asked on the test itself.

The Spanish Language Proficiency Test consists of 50 questions divided into two parts:

1. vocabulary questions
2. grammar questions (this part of the test is divided into three types of grammar questions)

Spanish Vocabulary Questions: Multiple Choice. The first part of the vocabulary test consists of multiple-choice questions. To test your knowledge of Spanish vocabulary, you will be asked to choose the most appropriate synonym for a particular word; you'll have five words from which to choose. This part of the test includes 20 vocabulary questions. Exhibit 5-4 shows a few examples from an actual test.

EXHIBIT 5-4. Sample Vocabulary Questions from the Spanish-Language Test

Find the suggested answer, of the five choices, that is closest in meaning to the key (*italicized*) word.

31. Yo *gocé de* la película anoche.
- **a.** aprendí de
- **b.** defendí de
- **c.** disfruté con
- **d.** aburrí con
- **e.** desagradé de

Find the suggested answer, of the five choices, that is closest in meaning to the key (*italicized*) word.

35. En el camino *encontramos* a muchas familias mexicanas que iban a pasar el domingo en Xochimilco.
- **a.** entendemos
- **b.** hallamos
- **c.** pedimos
- **d.** pegamos
- **e.** esperamos

Find the suggested answer, of the five choices, that is closest in meaning to the key (*italicized*) word.

42. ¿Donde está *el almacén?*
- **a.** el mueble
- **b.** la tienda
- **c.** la cocina
- **d.** la finca
- **e.** la puerta

Find the suggested answer, of the five choices, that is closest in meaning to the key (*italicized*) word.

45. Creo que no han llegado *todavía.*
- **a.** demasiado
- **b.** despacio
- **c.** aún
- **d.** antes
- **e.** después

Spanish Grammar Questions: Fill-in-the-Blanks. The grammar part of the Spanish Language Proficiency Test consists of three types of questions. The first set of grammar questions are in fill-in-the-blank format; there are 10 of these. Here, you will be asked to choose from five pairs of words or phrases that would fill each blank space so that the sentence makes sense. Exhibit 5-5 shows a few examples from this part of the Spanish grammar

EXHIBIT 5-5. Sample Grammar Questions from the Spanish Language Test

Fill-in-the-Blank Questions

Supply the correct words that should be used in place of the blanks within a sentence.

51. Porque no _____ Ud. cuando _____ pregunté sobre la maleta?
- **a.** contestaste, él
- **b.** contestó, yo
- **c.** contestó, él
- **d.** grita, nosotros
- **e.** escucharon, ellos

Supply the correct words that should be used in place of the blanks within a sentence.

52. Yo _____ levanto _____ seis.
- **a.** le, a las
- **b.** te, a la
- **c.** me, a las
- **d.** se, a la
- **e.** les, al

Supply the correct words that should be used in place of the blanks within a sentence.

60. ¿Cuánto _____ una camisa _____?
- **a.** valgo, nueva
- **b.** vela, nueva
- **c.** vale, nueva
- **d.** vale, nuevo
- **e.** vela, nuevo

test. As you can see, you really need to know your grammar well—for example, which nouns take feminine or masculine articles, when to use which type of pronoun (subject pronouns, direct object pronouns, indirect object pronouns, prepositional pronouns, and reflexive direct and indirect object pronouns), the correct position of words in a sentence, verb conjugations, and so on—in order to answer these questions correctly.

Fortunately, the U.S. Border Patrol's *Preparation Manual* does provide sample questions, with explanations regarding the correct answer and why the other response choices were incorrect. Furthermore, the LearningExpress book, *The Border Patrol Exam*, also provides a review of some essential grammatical rules, which can help you prepare even more for this part of the U.S. Border Patrol written exam.

Spanish Grammar Questions: Identifying Grammatically Incorrect Sentences. There are 12 questions in the second set of Spanish grammar questions. These questions will ask you to read carefully each of four sentences (per question), and then select the one sentence that is grammatically correct. Each of the other three sentences will be incorrect for some reason—for example,

- it uses an incorrect verb form
- it has an illogical structure
- it uses incorrect prepositions
- it includes incorrect terms
- it has misplaced clauses
- the verb tenses don't agree

Exhibit 5-6 shows you a few examples of this type of grammar question.

EXHIBIT 5-6. Sample Grammar Questions on the Spanish Language Test of the U.S. Border Patrol Exam

Identifying Grammatically Incorrect Sentences

61. Of the four choices given for each of the questions below, select the only one that is correct.
- **a.** Todo el mundo van al cine cada Sábado.
- **b.** Yo piense que tú no tienes razón.
- **c.** Es muy importante que los agentes sepan hablar espanol.
- **d.** ¿De donde estás Usted?

65. Of the four choices given for each of the questions below, select the only one that is correct.
- **a.** ¿Quién es el mejor jugo del equipo de fútbol?
- **b.** ¿Esperan Uds. ganar el campeonato el próximo año?
- **c.** Suelo estudio en la tarde.
- **d.** ¿Cómo se dice lo español?

69. Of the four choices given for each of the questions below, select the only one that is correct.
- **a.** Hay veinte repúblicas en la América Latina: México, las seis repúblicas de Centro-américa, Cuba, Haití, Santo Domingo, y las diez repúblicas de Sudamérica.
- **b.** La ciudad de México está la capital de la república.
- **c.** Chile es un país larga y estrecho.
- **d.** La Carretera Panamericana es importante porque el comercio y porque la defensa de las Américas.

Spanish Grammar Questions: Identifying the Right Word that Makes Sense in a Sentence. The third and final set of grammar questions consists of ten questions. Each question asks you to read a sentence carefully and then select the correct word or phrase to replace the *italicized* word or phrase of the sentence. You are given five possible responses from which to choose. Exhibit 5-7 shows some examples of this type of question.

EXHIBIT 5-7. Sample Grammar Questions from the Spanish Language Test

Identifying the Correct Word that Makes Sense in a Sentence

Read each sentence carefully, and supply, from the five choices, the word that will correctly replace the italicized word. If the italicized word is correct, choose answer **e.**

71. No es posible *lavar* el boleto aquí.
- **a.** cambiar
- **b.** cocinar
- **c.** abrazar
- **d.** enojar
- **e.** No es necesario hacer ninguna corrección.

Read each sentence carefully, and supply, from the five choices, the word that will correctly replace the italicized word. If the italicized word is correct, choose answer **e.**

73. ¿Quiere Ud. *escribe* al cine hoy, o tal vez mañana?
- **a.** va
- **b.** ir
- **c.** ve
- **d.** corre
- **e.** No es necesario hacer ninguna corrección.

Read each sentence carefully, and supply, from the five choices, the word that will correctly replace the italicized word. If the italicized word is correct, choose answer **e.**

79. Tengo *de* estudiar para un examen de español.
- **a.** pues
- **b.** que
- **c.** por
- **d.** a
- **e.** No es necesario hacer ninguna corrección.

THE ARTIFICIAL LANGUAGE TEST (ALT)

If you are not proficient in Spanish (or if you speak some Spanish but do not have a strong command of Spanish vocabulary and grammar), you should take the Artificial Language Test (ALT) instead of the Spanish Language Proficiency Test. The ALT is intended to test your *ability to learn* Spanish (or any language, but since Spanish is the language that is required for U.S. Border Patrol Agents, that's all we're concerned with here). You don't need to have any knowledge of any foreign language in order to do well on this test; you only need to show that you *can* learn a language.

As its name says, the ALT is based on an *artificial* language—and although this artificial language and this approach to testing may seem bizarre to you, the OPM and the Border Patrol Academy have studied the use of this test and determined it to be an *extremely effective predictor of success in learning Spanish at the Academy*.[1] The artificial language follows language rules that are based on the grammatical structures of languages that are derived from Latin (commonly known as the *Romance languages*), which include Italian, French, and of course Spanish (as well as other languages).

Think of the artificial language as a *code* that you are trying to decipher. The words themselves make no sense (after all, they're completely made up; for example, the word for *dog* might be *boglek*), but if you simply follow the rules of the language, which the test will give you, you can break the code and do well on the ALT.

Let's take a look at this mysterious artificial language—so it won't seem so mysterious. Exhibits 5-8 and 5-9 are lists of vocabulary words similar to what you will see on the test. (They're actually the same list, organized in different ways: Exhibit 5-8 lists them alphabetically by the English word, and Exhibit 5-9 lists them alphabetically by the artificial-language word.)

EXHIBIT 5-8. Sample Word List from the ALT

Arranged Alphabetically by the English Word

ENGLISH	ARTIFICIAL LANGUAGE	ENGLISH	ARTIFICIAL LANGUAGE
a, an	bex	skillful	janle
alien	huslek	that	velle
and	loa	the	wir
boy	ekaplek	this	volle
country	failek	to be	synker
difficult	glasle	to border	regker
enemy	avelek	to cross	chonker
friend	kometlek	to drive	arker
from	mor	to escape	pirker
government	almanlek	to guard	bonker
he, him	yev	to have	tulker
jeep	daqlek	to identify	kalenker
legal	colle	to injure	liaker
loyal	inle	to inspect	zelker
man	kaplek	to shoot	degker
of	quea	to spy	tatker
paper	trenedlek	to station	lexker
river	browlek	to work	frigker

EXHIBIT 5-9. Sample Word List from the ALT

Arranged Alphabetically by the Artificial Language Word

ARTIFICIAL LANGUAGE	ENGLISH	ARTIFICIAL LANGUAGE	ENGLISH
almanlek	government	kaplek	man
arker	to drive	kometlek	friend
avelek	enemy	lexker	to station
bex	a, an	liaker	to injure
bonker	to guard	loa	and
browlek	river	mor	from
chonker	to cross	pirker	to escape
colle	legal	quea	of
daqlek	jeep	regker	to border
degker	to shoot	synker	to be
ekaplek	boy	tatker	to spy
failek	country	trenedlek	paper
frigker	to work	tulker	to have
glasle	difficult	velle	that
huslek	alien	volle	this
inle	loyal	wir	the
janle	skillful	yev	he, him
kalenker	to identify	zelker	to inspect

Now let's look at a few examples to show how this language (or code) works. As shown in the vocabulary list in Exhibit 5-8, the word for *a* in the artificial language is *bex*, and the word for *boy* is *ekaplek*. Thus, *a boy* translates to *bex ekaplek*, just as you would translate it into other languages:

- In Spanish, *a boy* is *el niño*.
- In French, *a boy* is *le garçon*.
- In Italian, *a boy* is *il ragazzo*.
- In the artificial language, *a boy* is *bex ekaplek*.

See how easy it is? You simply need to follow the grammatical rules of the artificial language, which are also provided on the test itself. Exhibit 5-10 shows a sample rule. Note, however, that this may *not* be one of the *actual* rules you will be given on the written exam you take; instead, this rule is simply an example of the *type* of information you will receive.

The ALT is composed of four parts:

- Part 1 consists of 20 questions.
- Part 2 consists of 10 questions.
- Part 3 consists of 12 questions.
- Part 4 consists of 8 questions.

EXHIBIT 5-10. Sample Grammatical Rule for the Artificial Language

Rule 1:

To form the feminine singular of a noun, a pronoun, or an adjective, add the suffix *-nef* to the masculine singular form. Only nouns, pronouns, adjectives, and articles take feminine endings in the Artificial Language. When gender is not specified, the masculine form is used.

Example: If a male eagle is a *verlek*, then a female eagle is a *verleknef*.

If an ambitious man is a *tosle* man, an ambitious woman is a *toslenef* woman.

From *Border Patrol Exam: The Complete Preparation Guide, Third Edition*, page 66; New York: Learning Express, LLC, 2006.

Just as the Spanish Language Proficiency Test consists of 50 questions on vocabulary and grammar, the ALT also consists of a total of 50 questions, all of which are multiple-choice, with five answer choices each. Let's look at each part of the ALT individually.

ALT Part 1: 20 Questions. This part tests your ability to translate words accurately, from English to the Artificial Language (and vice versa). Exhibit 5-11 shows two sample questions.

Exhibit 5-11. Sample Questions from Part 1 of the ALT

31. Sentence — Translation
She is an alien. — Yev synem bex huslek.
(numbered words: 1 = Yev, 2 = synem, 3 = huslek)

a. *Only* the word numbered 1 is correctly translated.
b. *Only* the word numbered 2 is correctly translated.
c. *Only* the word numbered 3 is correctly translated.
d. *Two* or *more* of the numbered words are correctly translated.
e. *None* of the numbered words is correctly translated.

32. Sentence — Translation
The guard is a friend. — Wir bonlek synem bex kometlek.
(numbered words: 1 = Wir, 2 = bonlek, 3 = kometlek)

a. *Only* the word numbered 1 is correctly translated.
b. *Only* the word numbered 2 is correctly translated.
c. *Only* the word numbered 3 is correctly translated.
d. *Two* or *more* of the numbered words are correctly translated.
e. *None* of the numbered words is correctly translated.

ALT Part 2: 10 Questions. The questions on this part of the ALT test your ability not only to translate words from English into the Artificial Language but also to show other language skills—including (but not limited to) these:

- using the correct article (masculine or feminine) for each noun
- using the correct noun form (whether it is singular or plural)
- using the correct tense of a verb (present, past, future, and so on)
- conjugating verbs correctly, to ensure that the form of the verb matches the pronoun or noun

Exhibit 5-12 provides a couple of sample questions for this part of the ALT.

EXHIBIT 5-12. Sample Questions from Part 2 of the ALT

51. The men and women who patrol and
- **a.** kaplekoz loa kaplekferoz
- **b.** kaplekoz loa kapleknefoz
- **c.** kaplekae loa kapleknefae
- **d.** kaplekae loa kaplekferae
- **e.** kaplekoz bex kaplekferoz

52. guard the border have a complex and difficult job.
- **a.** bonimoz wir reglek
- **b.** bonimoz wir reglekoz
- **c.** bonem wir reglek
- **d.** bonker wir reglek
- **e.** bonim wir reglek

ALT Part 3: 12 Questions. The questions in this part of the ALT test also test your ability to choose the correct form of nouns, verbs, adjectives, and adverbs. Exhibit 5-13 shows two examples.

EXHIBIT 5-13. Sample Questions from Part 3 of the ALT

61. Velleoz (boys escaped).
- **a.** ekaplekoz pirzotim
- **b.** ekaplekoz pirkerim
- **c.** ekaplekim pirzotim
- **d.** ekaplekim pirkerim
- **e.** ekaplekae pirzotim

62. Wir kapleknefoz (drove skillfully).
- **a.** arzotnefim janlekinef
- **b.** arzotnefim janlekinefoz
- **c.** arzotim janlekinef
- **d.** arzotim janleki
- **e.** arzotim janlekinefoz

ALT Part 4: 8 Questions. The questions in this final part of the ALT ask you to translate a word or several words into the correct tense or form. Exhibit 5-14 provides a couple of examples.

EXHIBIT 5-14. Sample Questions from Part 4 of the ALT

79. Velle almanlek *fertulem fercolleki* zelzotem *yevnef* trenedlekoz. (negative present tense singular—negative adverb—possessive feminine pronoun)
a. tulem—fercolleki—yevnef
b. fertulem—fercolleki—yevnef
c. tulem—fercolleki—yevnefae
d. fertulem—fercolleki—yevnefae
e. fertulem—fercollenefki—yevnefae

80. Vellenefoz *fercolle huslekae deglekoz* liazotim wir ekaplekoz. (negative feminine plural adjective—possessive feminine plural noun—plural noun)
a. fercollenef—huslekae—deglekoz
b. fercolle—huslekae—deglekoz
c. fercolle—husleknefae—deglekoz
d. fercollenefoz—husleknefozae—deglekoz
e. fercollenefoz—husleknefozae—degleknefoz

HOW TO PREPARE FOR THE EXAM

As you can see from the examples provided in this chapter, the Border Patrol Exam isn't easy. Therefore, to prepare for the test, you should take advantage of as much information you can find out about the test *before* you take it, and you should answer as many practice questions as you can find.

The Preparation Manual for the U.S. Border Patrol Test. This manual is a 60-page PDF (which, again, you can download at this web site: www.tsa

.gov/assets/pdf/soar/preparation_manual_bpa.pdf. Here's a quick overview of the information you can find in these 60 pages.

- one page of test-taking tips
- ten pages of information about the Logical Reasoning Test for example,
  - advice on educated guessing
  - how to read the questions so you can interpret them correctly when answering
  - insight into various types of questions (such as questions that ask you about *all* people, situations, or events—or the opposite: *none* or *not* questions—and reasoning based on *if-then* questions)
- a three-page Logical Reasoning practice test, consisting of eight practice questions for this part of the exam
- four pages of explanation of the correct (and incorrect) answers on the Logical Reasoning practice test
- six pages of 16 sample questions for the Spanish Language Proficiency Test (four questions from each of the vocabulary and three grammar sections); since explanations of the correct and incorrect answers for each question are given immediately following the question, this is not a true practice test)
- 33 pages (about half of the *Preparation Manual*) devoted to the Artificial Language Test; including
  - the vocabulary lists
  - the grammar rules
  - a glossary of grammatical terms (as a refresher course to what you learned in grade-school and high-school English)
  - a six-page practice test comprising 50 questions (the same number that will be featured on your actual test)
  - 18 pages of detailed explanations about the correct and incorrect answers for each of the 50 questions

LearningExpress's Border Patrol Exam: The Complete Preparation Guide. If you feel you need more information and help preparing and studying for the exam than the CBP's free download provides, consider getting a copy of one of the many test-prep guides available. In addition to ours, described here, others are listed in Appendix C. Our book contains 180 pages of information (prepared with the assistance of a Border Patrol Agent with 13 years' experience) including

- study schedules, depending on how much time you have before you take the test
- information on process-of-elimination techniques and educated guessing, to help you answer questions
- extensive guidelines on how to tackle each part of the test
- sample questions for each part of the test, with very detailed explanations of the correct and incorrect answers
- two complete practice exams (30 pages each, comparable to what the actual test looks like), with sample answer sheets
- 24 pages of detailed explanations of the correct and incorrect answers to each question on both exams (12 pages of explanation for each exam)
- free access to an online Border Patrol practice exam, which you can take at www.learningexpressfreeoffer.com, with a pass code you will receive in the copy of the book you buy
- free access to your score on that online test, which will show you in which areas of the test you need to study more and spend more time preparing for that part of the exam

Good luck!

CHAPTER six

A HISTORY OF THE U.S. BORDER PATROL

THERE HAS been a border patrol in the United States for about 200 years, although the organization as we now know it wasn't formed until 1924. The unofficial border patrol in the early 1800s was intended to protect landowners in Texas along the border with Mexico. But curiously, the first group of illegal immigrants that the United States sought to limit were the Chinese, at the end of the nineteenth century. This final chapter provides details on those events in the history of the Border Patrol—and more. You don't really *need* to know anything in this chapter in order to apply to or be hired by the Border Patrol, but if you're interested in how the agency has evolved, read on!

THE FIRST BORDER PATROL AGENTS: THE TEXAS RANGERS

The first border patrolmen (and they *were* men) in the United States were the Texas Rangers, who starting protecting the border between Texas and Mexico in the early 1800s, because there was no regular army to protect the 300 or so families who had settled near the Gulf of Mexico.[1] Stephen Austin (who was known as the father of Texas) created the first corps of border patrollers in 1823, and he was the one who first called them Rangers, because their duties required them to range over the entire country.

In 1836, the Congress of the Texas Republic (which existed from 1836 to 1845) passed a law enabling its president, Sam Houston, to create a battalion of 280 mounted riflemen to protect the frontier. Up until 1840, the Rangers typically protected against Indians. But in 1842, President Houston approved a law for a company of mounted men to act as Rangers on the state's Mexican border.

In 1861, Texas seceded from the Union and joined the Confederacy, but it was readmitted to the United States in 1870. In 1874, the Texas Rangers were organized into six companies, with 75 men per company; they patrolled across Texas, partly as soldiers and partly as police officers.

The Texas Rangers still exist today, but they are part of the Texas Department of Public Safety, which is a state-level law-enforcement organization.

THE FIRST IMMIGRATION LAWS

It was also during the 1880s that Congress first started passing laws limiting immigration, to stop the flow of what seems to us today an unusual group of immigrants: the Chinese, who came to this country to work, and threatened our own labor market because they worked cheaply. During the first 100 years after the United States was formed, the country hadn't been much concerned with protecting its borders. But from the 1880s on, border security would become more of an issue.

Interestingly, the term *alien* first surfaced during the discussion on whether to pass the Fouteenth Amendment (proposed in 1866 and ratified in 1868) to the U.S. Constitution. This amendment is one of the post-Civil War Reconstruction Amendments, and its original intent was to secure the rights of former slaves. Section 1 of the Amendment states as follows:

> All persons born or naturalized in the United States, and subject to the jurisdiction thereof, are citizens of the United States and of the State wherein they reside. No State shall make or enforce any law which shall abridge the privileges or immunities of citizens of the United States; nor shall any State deprive any person of life, liberty, or prosperity, without due process of law; nor deny to any person within its jurisdiction the equal protection of the laws.[2]

Ironically, the rights of Native Americans were ignored. In 1884, the Supreme Court ruled that the children born to Native American parents were not citizens, even if they were born in the United States.

TIMELINE OF KEY EVENTS IN THE HISTORY OF U.S. BORDER PROTECTION

Here's a timeline of key events in the history of border protection in the United States:[3]

- **1875: The Right to Regulate Immigration.** The U.S. Supreme Court ruled that the federal government had the exclusive right to regulate immigration.
- **1882–1891: First Laws Limiting Immigration.** Congress started passing laws severely limiting immigration, including the Chinese Exclusion Act of 1882, which was intended to protect the U.S. labor market from the Chinese and other groups of cheap labor. The Immigration Act of 1882 charged a tax on every immigrant and prevented the entry of *convicts, idiots, lunatics, and persons likely to become a public charge. The list of persons who were excluded expanded quickly, and immigration law became increasingly complex.*[4]

  In 1885 and 1887, Congress passed two Alien Contract Labor laws to further bar certain workers from immigrating. The increasingly restrictive laws prompted a growing number of migrants to attempt illegal entry, creating the need for an official border-control presence.

In 1891, a federal agency was created to administer immigration laws. This agency evolved into the Immigration and Naturalization Service (the INS) in 1933.

- **1904: First Inspectors to Patrol U.S. Borders.** The U.S. Immigration Service assigned a few mounted inspectors to patrol the border to prevent illegal crossings. Because they were really just a token force and because they had no real training in border patrol, these officers weren't very effective: authorities were unable to stem the tide of illegal aliens crossing U.S. borders.
- **1915: Increased Number of Border Guards.** In March 1915, Congress authorized a separate group of inspectors, called mounted guards or mounted inspectors, who operated from El Paso, Texas. There were only about 75 of these at any one time, and they rode on horseback and patrolled as far west as California. The focus of these inspectors was the Chinese immigrants who were trying to avoid the Chinese Exclusion laws passed 33 years earlier.
- **1917: Restricting Immigration.** In an attempt to restrict the number of immigrants entering the United States, the country passed the Immigration Act of 1917, which placed a head tax of $8 on each immigrant and required all immigrants to pass a literacy test. Section 8 of this act also prohibited smuggling, harboring, concealing, or assisting a migrant who was not properly admitted by an immigration inspector or not lawfully entitled to enter or reside in the United States.

  Before this act was passed, Mexicans and Canadians were able to cross into the United States at will and without restrictions. During the Mexican Revolution and World War I (1910–1920), troops stationed along the border had greatly reduced illegal border activity. After World War I, however, with the soldiers gone, illegal immigrant crossings increased.
- **1920: Prohibition and Illegal Smuggling of Alcohol.** On January 16, 1920, Congress passed the Eighteenth Amendment to the U.S. Constitution, prohibiting the importation, transport, manufacture, or sale of alcoholic beverages; this was the beginning of Prohibition. Al-

though this might not seem related to what we think of nowadays as a border issue, smuggling liquor into the country from both Canada and Mexico actually demanded most of the attention of the Border Patrol effort at this time. Bootleggers smuggled alcohol from Mexico by crossing the Rio Grande River, not over the bridges, but with pack mules.

- **1921 and 1924: New Laws to Restrict Immigration from Europe.** Congress passed new Immigration Acts because of increasing concern that there would be a huge wave of immigrants coming from Europe—people who were trying to escape the ravages wrought by The Great War (which we now know as World War I). Unfortunately, these limits on lawful immigration also led to increased unlawful immigration.
- **1924: Creation of the Border Patrol.** On May 28, 1924, Congress established the U.S. Border Patrol as part of the Immigration Bureau, an arm of the Department of Labor. This Patrol recruited many of the early force of 450 officers from the Texas Rangers and local sheriffs and their deputies, because they knew the land and the dangers it presented. These Agents received a badge, a revolver, and an annual salary of $1,680. Recruits provided their own horses and saddles (although the U.S. government did supply oats and hay for the horses). In December 1924, Congress authorized the purchase of uniforms for the Border Patrol.

  This small group of officers was responsible for enforcing Section 8 of the Immigration Act of 1917, which (as stated above) prohibited smuggling, harboring, concealing, or assisting a migrant who was not duly admitted by an immigration officer or not lawfully entitled to enter or reside in the United States. *This was really the beginning of the Border Patrol as we know it today.*
- **1925: Expansion of Border Patrol Areas.** Patrol areas were expanded to include more than 2,000 miles of seacoast extending along the Gulf and Florida coasts.
- **1932: Focus on Mexico and Canada.** The Border Patrol was placed under the authority of two directors. One was in charge of the Mexican border office at El Paso, Texas; the other was in charge of the Canadian border office at Detroit, Michigan.

- **1933: Creation of the INS.** The INS was created from the federal agency formed in 1891. Originally part of the U.S. Department of Labor, it was later moved to the Justice Department. In March 2003, the INS was absorbed into and replaced by the U.S. Citizenship and Immigration Services (USCIS), which currently comprises 15,000 federal employees and contractors who work in approximately 250 offices around the world, and who are primarily *responsible for the administration of immigration and naturalization adjudication functions and establishing immigration services policies and priorities.*[5] The USCIS is part of the Department of Homeland Security, which was created in 2002.
- **1934: Recognition of the Need for Border Patrol Training.** The first Border Patrol Academy opened at Camp Chigas in El Paso, Texas, because the Border Patrol recognized that formal training was needed; 34 trainees attended classes in marksmanship and horsemanship. Because Border Patrol Agents typically work in and patrol rugged terrain and need quick and quiet transportation, horses remain essential transportation for agents even to the present day.
- **World War II: Increased Number of Border Patrol Agents.** The Border Patrol added 712 agents and 57 auxiliary personnel, bringing the force to 1,531 officers, to allay the American public's fears that aliens would undermine the country's security and try to enter the United States. During the war, the Border Patrol provided tighter control of the border, worked in alien detention camps, guarded diplomats, and assisted the U.S. Coast Guard in searching for enemy spies. It was also during the war that the Border Patrol began to use aircraft, which became an integral part of operations.
- **1942: Mexican Nationals Invited to Immigrate to Work as Farm Laborers.** On August 4, 1942, the United States made an agreement with Mexico to provide for the importation of Mexican nationals because U.S. farm laborers had entered the military or had found jobs in the expanding war industry during World War II. This had created an acute labor shortage in agriculture, and food production was critical to the war effort. But the importation of alien labor did not end when the war ended, and over the next 14 years, the U.S. agricultural industry imported laborers from Mexico, the British West Indies, and Canada.

- **1952: Deportation of Mexican Immigrants.** The U.S. government airlifted 52,000 illegal immigrants back to the Mexican interior, because citizen groups alleged that the huge number of illegal migrants, especially in the California and Rio Grande Valley areas along the Mexican border, was responsible for the growing violent crime rate.
- **1952: New Classification of Immigrants.** The Immigration and Nationality Act of 1952 (INA) was passed. It continues to be the basic immigration law in the United States, although it has changed considerably since it was enacted. Essentially, the INA originally defined three types of immigrants:
  1. immigrants with special skills or relatives of U.S. citizens who were exempt from quotas and who were to be admitted without restrictions
  2. average immigrants whose numbers were not to exceed 270,000 per year
  3. refugees

  Also, the INA allowed the U.S. government to deport immigrants or naturalized citizens engaged in subversive activities, and to prevent suspected subversives from entering the United States.
- **Late 1950s to Early 1960s: Border Patrol Agents First Assigned to Airplanes.** Because significant numbers of illegal migrants began entering the United States on private aircraft, President John F. Kennedy ordered Border Patrol Agents to accompany domestic flights to prevent takeovers by hijackers. During this time period, the Border Patrol also began assisting other agencies in intercepting illegal drugs en route from Mexico.
- **1980s to 1990s: Use of Better Technology.** Because of a tremendous increase in illegal immigration to the United States, the Border Patrol increased its staffing and implemented more current technology, including infrared night-vision scopes, seismic sensors, and a modern computer processing system, all of which helped the Border Patrol locate, apprehend, and process those crossing into the United States illegally.
- **1990: Immigration Law Reform.** The Immigration Act of 1990 significantly reformed U.S. immigration laws by allocating visas among foreign countries more evenly than in the past, and by fostering

increased legal immigration to the United States. It also opened a lottery program that assigns approximately 50,000 visas each year to people born in countries with low immigration rates to the United States.

- **1993: Operation Hold the Line.** Border Patrol agents and technology were concentrated in specific areas, providing a show of force to deter illegal border crossings near El Paso, Texas. Then the Border Patrol expanded this effort to San Diego, California, which accounted for more than half of illegal entries.
- **1994: Operation Gatekeeper.** This operation was implemented in San Diego, California, and reduced illegal entries there by more than 75% over the next few years.

THE CREATION OF THE DEPARTMENT OF HOMELAND SECURITY

On October 8, 2001, five weeks after the 9/11 terrorist attacks on New York City and Washington, DC, President Bush created the White House Office of Homeland Security. A year later, on November 19, 2002, Congress passed legislation mandating the Department of Homeland Security; the DHS became operational three months after that, on January 24, 2003; and most agencies comprising the new department merged on March 1, 2003. The Border Patrol was one of the agencies folded into the newly created Department of Homeland Security.

This was the largest reorganization of the federal government since the U.S. Department of Defense was created 60 years ago, in 1947. The DHS merged 22 agencies, including the U.S. Customs Service (which had been part of the Treasury Department) and the INS (which had been part of the Justice Department). The functions of those agencies are now handled by

- ***CBP: The U.S. Customs and Border Protection Agency***, which has responsibility for inspection of borders and ports of entry
- ***ICE: The U.S. Immigrations and Customs Enforcement Agency***, which has responsibility for customs law enforcement and immigration law enforcement, including detention and removal of illegal aliens, as well as intelligence and investigations.[6]

Homeland Security leverages resources within federal, state, and local governments, coordinating the transition of multiple agencies into a single, integrated agency that is focused on protecting the United States and its citizens. More than 87,000 different governmental jurisdictions at the federal, state, and local level have homeland security responsibilities.[7] Exhibit 6-1 lists the major components that currently comprise the DHS.

EXHIBIT 6-1. Components of the Department of Homeland Security

- The *Directorate for National Protection and Programs* works to advance the Department's risk-reduction mission. Reducing risk requires an integrated approach that encompasses both physical and virtual threats and their associated human elements.
- The *Directorate for Science and Technology* is the primary research and development arm of the Department. It provides federal, state, and local officials with the technology and capabilities to protect the homeland.
- The *Directorate for Management* is responsible for Department budgets and appropriations, expenditure of funds, accounting and finance, procurement, human resources, information technology systems, facilities and equipment, and the identification and tracking of performance measurements.
- The *Office of Policy* is the primary policy formulation and coordination component for the Department of Homeland Security. It provides a centralized, coordinated focus to the development of Department-wide, long-range planning to protect the United States.
- The *Office of Health Affairs* coordinates all medical activities of the Department of Homeland Security to ensure appropriate preparation for and response to incidents having medical significance.
- The *Office of Intelligence and Analysis* is responsible for using information and intelligence from multiple sources to identify and assess current and future threats to the United States.
- The *Office of Operations Coordination* is responsible for monitoring the security of the United States on a daily basis and coordinating activities within the Department and with governors, Homeland Security Advisors, law-enforcement partners, and critical infrastructure operators in all 50 states and more than 50 major urban areas nationwide.

(Continued)

EXHIBIT 6-1. Continued

- The *Federal Law Enforcement Training Center* provides career-long training to law enforcement professionals to help them fulfill their responsibilities safely and proficiently.

- The *Domestic Nuclear Detection Office* works to enhance the nuclear detection efforts of federal, state, territorial, tribal, and local governments, and the private sector, and to ensure a coordinated response to such threats.

- The *Transportation Security Administration (TSA)* protects the nation's transportation systems to ensure freedom of movement for people and commerce.

- *United States Customs and Border Protection (CBP)* is responsible for protecting our nation's borders in order to prevent terrorists and terrorist weapons from entering the United States, while facilitating the flow of legitimate trade and travel.

- *United States Citizenship and Immigration Services (USCIS)* is responsible for the administration of immigration and naturalization adjudication functions and establishing immigration services policies and priorities.

- *United States Immigration and Customs Enforcement (ICE)*, the largest investigative arm of the Department of Homeland Security, is responsible for identifying and shutting down vulnerabilities in the nation's border, economic, transportation, and infrastructure security.

- The *United States Coast Guard (USCG)* protects the public, the environment, and U.S. economic interests in the nation's ports and waterways, along the coast, on international waters, or in any maritime region as required to support national security.

- The *Federal Emergency Management Agency (FEMA)* prepares the nation for hazards, manages federal response and recovery efforts following any national incident, and administers the National Flood Insurance Program.

- The *United States Secret Service* protects the president and other high-level officials and investigates counterfeiting and other financial crimes, including financial institution fraud, identity theft, computer fraud, and computer-based attacks on our nation's financial, banking, and telecommunications infrastructure.

From www.dhs.gov/xabout/structure/.

Appendix A

Colleges and Universities That Offer Four-year Bachelor's Degrees in Criminal Justice and Law Enforcement[1]

Listed alphabetically by state and then by college or university

Alabama

Columbia Southern University
Orange Beach, AL
www.columbiasouthern.edu

Judson College
Marion, AL
www.judson.edu

Samford University*
Birmingham, AL
www.samford.edu

Virginia College at Huntsville
Huntsville, AL
www.vc.edu

Alaska

None that offer BA degrees

Arizona

Arizona State University* West
Phoenix, AZ
www.west.asu.edu

Northcentral University
Prescott Valley, AZ
www.ncu.edu

Northern Arizona University
Flagstaff, AZ
www.nau.edu

University of Arizona
Tucson, AZ
www.arizona.edu

University of Phoenix
Phoenix, AZ
www.phoenix.edu

An * denotes a college included in *The Best 366 Colleges, 2008 Edition*, published by The Princeton Review.

Arkansas

University of Arkansas, Fort Smith
Fort Smith, AR
www.uafortsmith.edu

California

California Baptist University
Riverside, CA
www.calbaptist.edu

California State University
www.calstate.edu

Dominguez Hills Campus
Carson, CA
www.csudh.edu

East Bay Campus
Hayward, CA
www.csueastbay.edu

Los Angeles Campus
Los Angeles, CA
www.calstatela.edu

San Bernardino Campus
San Bernardino, CA
www.csusb.edu

National University
San Diego, CA
www.nu.edu

San Diego State University
San Diego, CA
www.sdsu.edu

Sonoma State University*
Rohnert Park, CA
www.sonoma.edu

Westwood College of Technology
Los Angeles, CA
www.westwood.edu

Colorado

Johnson & Wales University
Denver, CO
www.jwu.edu

Metropolitan State College of Denver
Denver, CO
www.mscd.edu

University of Colorado, Colorado Springs
Colorado Springs, CO
www.uccs.edu

Westwood College of Technology, Denver South
Denver, CO
www.westwood.edu

Connecticut

Sacred Heart University
Fairfield, CT
www.sacredheart.edu

University of New Haven
West Haven, CT
www.newhaven.edu

Delaware

None that offer BA degrees

District of Columbia

Trinity Washington University
Washington, DC
www.trinitydc.edu

Florida

Bethune-Cookman University
Daytona Beach, CA
www.cookman.edu

Edward Waters College
Jacksonville, FL
www.ewc.edu

Everest University, Brandon
Tampa, FL
www.everest.edu

Johnson & Wales University, North Miami
North Miami, FL
www.jwu.edu

Keiser University
Fort Lauderdale, FL (Main Campus)
www.keiseruniversity.edu

Lynn University
Boca Raton, FL
www.lynn.edu

Remington College, Tampa
Tampa, FL
www.remingtoncollege.edu/tampa

Southeastern University
Lakeland, FL
www.seuniversity.edu

Georgia

Bauder College
Atlanta, GA
www.bauder.edu

Georgia College and State University
Milledgeville, GA
www.gcsu.edu

Hawaii

Hawaii Pacific University
Honolulu, HI
www.hpu.edu

University of Hawaii, West Oahu
Pearl City, HI
www.uhwo.edu

Idaho

Boise State University
Boise, ID
www.boisestate.edu

Illinois

Bradley University*
Peoria, IL
www.bradley.edu

Concordia University
Chicago, IL
www.cuchicago.edu

Eureka College
Eureka, IL
www.eureka.edu

Greenville College
Greenville, IL
www.greenville.edu

Lewis University
Romeoville, IL
www.lewisu.edu

Millikin University
Decatur, IL
www.millikin.edu

Southern Illinois University, Carbondale
Carbondale, IL
www.siu.edu

Western Illinois University
Moline, IL
www.wiu.edu

Western Illinois University, Quad Cities
Moline, IL
www.wiu.edu/qc

Westwood College of Technology
Chicago, IL
www.westwood.edu

Indiana

Indiana Business College

Fort Wayne Campus
Fort Wayne, IN
www.ibcshools.edu

Indianapolis Campus
Indianapolis, IN
www.ibcschools.edu

Muncie Campus
Muncie, IN
www.ibcschools.edu

Indiana Institute of Technology
Fort Wayne, IN
www.indianatech.edu

Indiana University-Purdue University, Fort Wayne
Fort Wayne, IN
www.iupui.edu

Purdue University
West Lafayette, IN
www.purdue.edu

Purdue University, Calumet
Hammond, IN
www.calumet.purdue.edu

University of Indianapolis
Indianapolis IN
www.uindy.edu

Iowa

Briar Cliff University
Sioux City, IA
www.briarcliff.edu

Kaplan University, Mason City
Mason City, IA
www.kucampus.edu

Mount Mercy College
Cedar Rapids, IA
www.mtmercy.edu

Kansas

Central Christian College of Kansas
McPherson, KS
www.centralchristian.edu

MidAmerica Nazarene University
Olathe, KS
www.mnu.edu

Newman University
Wichita, KS
www.newmanu.edu

Washburn University
Topeka, KS
www.washburn.edu

Kentucky

Beckfield College
Florence, KY
www.beckfield.edu

Bellarmine University*
Louisville, KY
www.bellarmine.edu

Campbellsville University
Campbellsville, KY
www.campbellsville.edu

Thomas More College
Crestview Hills, KY
www.thomasmore.edu

Union College
Barbourville, KY
www.unionky.edu

University of Louisville
Louisville, KY
www.louisville.edu

Louisiana

Louisiana College
Pineville, LA
www.lacollege.edu

Southwest University
Kenner, LA
www.southwest.edu

Maine

Husson College
Bangor, ME
www.husson.edu

Thomas College
Waterville, ME
www.thomas.edu

University of Maine*
Augusta, ME
www.uma.edu

Maryland

Frostburg State University
Frederick, MD
www.frostburg.edu

Massachusetts

American International College
Springfield, MA
www.aic.edu

Lasell College
Newton, MA
www.lasell.edu

Newbury College
Boston, MA
www.newbury.edu

Salem State College
Salem, MA
www.salemstate.edu

Springfield College
Springfield, MA
www.spfldcol.edu

Suffolk University*
Boston, MA
www.suffolk.edu

University of Massachusetts*
Amherst, MA
www.umass.edu

Michigan

Concordia University
Ann Arbor, MI
www.cuaa.edu

Grand Valley State University
Allendale, MI
www.gvsu.edu

Lake Superior State University
Sault Ste. Marie, MI
www.lssu.edu

Michigan State University*
East Lansing, MI
www.msu.edu

University of Detroit Mercy
Detroit, MI
www.udmercy.edu

University of Michigan, Flint
Flint, MI
www.umflint.edu

Minnesota

Concordia University, St. Paul
St. Paul, MN
www.csp.edu

Minnesota State University, Mankato
Mankato, MN
www.mnsu.edu

St. Mary's University of Minnesota
Minneapolis, MN
www.smumn.edu

Southwest Minnesota State University
Marshall, MN
www.southwest.msus.edu

Winona State University
Winona, MN
www.winona.edu

Mississippi

Mississippi College
Clinton, MS
www.mc.edu

University of Mississippi*
Lafayette, MS
www.olemiss.edu

Missouri

Central Methodist University
Fayette, MO
www.centralmethodist.edu

Columbia College
Columbia, MO
www.ccis.edu

Culver-Stockton College
Canton, MO
www.culver.edu

Grantham University
Kansas City, MO
www.grantham.edu

Hannibal-LaGrange College
Hannibal, MO
www.hlg.edu

Harris-Stowe State University
St. Louis, MO
www.hssu.edu

Lincoln University
Jefferson City, MO
www.lincolnu.edu

Missouri Southern State University
Joplin, MO
www.mssu.edu

Missouri Valley College
Marshall, MO
www.moval.edu

Park University
Parkville, MO
www.park.edu

Saint Louis University*
St. Louis, MO
www.slu.edu

Southwest Baptist University
Bolivar, MO
www.sbuniv.edu

University of Central Missouri
Warrensburg, MO
www.ucmo.edu

University of Missouri, Kansas City
Kansas City, MO
www.umkc.edu

Montana

None that offer BA degrees

Nebraska

Bellevue University
Bellevue, NE
www.bellevue.edu

Dana College
Blair, NE
www.dana.edu

Peru State College
Peru, NE
www.peru.edu

Nevada

None that offer BA degrees

New Hampshire

Granite State College
Concord, NH
www.granite.edu

Hesser College
Manchester, NH (and other campuses)
www.hesser.edu

New Jersey

The College of New Jersey*
Ewing, NJ
www.tcnj.edu

Georgian Court University
Lakewood, NJ
www.georgian.edu

Kean University
Union, NJ
www.kean.edu

Rutgers, The State University of New Jersey*
New Brunswick, NJ
www.rutgers.edu

Thomas Edison State College
Trenton, NJ
www.tesc.edu

New Mexico

Western New Mexico University
Silver City, NM
www.wnmu.edu

New York

Adelphi University
Garden City, NY
www.adelphi.edu

City University of New York, John Jay College of Criminal Justice
New York, NY
www.jjay.cuny.edu

College of Saint Rose
Albany, NY
www.strose.edu

Iona College
New Rochelle, NY
www.iona.edu

Keuka College
Keuka Park, NY
www.keuka.edu

Long Island University, C.W. Post Campus
Brookville, NY
www.liu.edu

Marist College*
Poughkeepsie, NY
www.marist.edu

Mercy College
New York, NY (and other campuses)
www.mercycollege.edu

Molloy College
Rockville Centre, NY
www.molloy.edu

Monroe College
Bronx, NY (and other campuses)
www.monroecollege.edu

New York Institute of Technology
New York, NY (and other campuses)
www.nyit.edu

Pace University
New York, NY
www.pace.edu

Roberts Wesleyan College
Rochester, NY
www.roberts.edu

Rochester Institute of Technology*
Rochester, NY
www.rit.edu

Sage College of Albany
Troy and Albany, NY
www.sage.edu

St. John's University*
Queens, NY
www.stjohns.edu

St. Thomas Aquinas College
Sparkill, NY
www.stac.edu

State University of New York, Canton
Canton, NY
www.canton.edu

North Carolina

Brevard College
Brevard, NC
www.brevard.edu

Catawba College*
Salisbury, NC
www.catawba.edu

Chowan University
Murfreesboro, NC
www.chowan.edu

Miller-Motte Technical College
Wilmington, NC
www.miller-motte.com

North Carolina Central University
Durham, NC
www.nccu.edu

Surry Community College
Dobson, NC
www.surry.edu

North Dakota

University of Mary
Bismarck, ND
www.umary.edu

Ohio

Ashland University
Ashland, OH
www.ashland.edu

Cedarville University
Cedarville, OH
www.cedarville.edu

Heidelberg College
Tiffin, OH
www.heidelberg.edu

Lake Erie College
Painesville, OH
www.lec.edu

Ohio Northern University*
Ada, OH
www.onu.edu

Tiffin University
Tiffin, OH
www.tiffin.edu

Union Institute & University
Cincinnati, OH
www.tui.edu

University of Findlay
Findlay, OH
www.findlay.edu

Urbana University
Urbana, OH
www.urbana.edu

Youngstown State University
Youngstown, OH
www.ysu.edu

Oklahoma

Mid-America Christian University
Oklahoma City, OK
www.macu.edu

Northeastern State University
Tahlequah, OK
www.nsuok.edu

Oklahoma City University
Oklahoma City, OK
www.okcu.edu

Rogers State University
Claremore, OK
www.rsu.edu

Oregon

Portland State University
Portland, OR
www.pdx.edu

Southern Oregon University
Ashland, OR
www.sou.edu

Western Oregon University
Monmouth, OR
www.wou.edu

Pennsylvania

Alvernia College
Reading, PA
www.alvernia.edu

Chestnut Hill College
Philadelphia, PA
www.chc.edu

Delaware Valley College
Doylestown, PA
www.delval.edu

Drexel University*
Philadelphia, PA
www.drexel.edu

Gwynedd-Mercy College
Gwynedd Valley, PA
www.gmc.edu

Keystone College
La Plume, PA
www.keystone.edu

Lock Haven University of Pennsylvania
Lock Haven, PA
www.lhup.edu

Mansfield University of Pennsylvania
Mansfield, PA
www.mansfield.edu

Marywood University
Scranton, PA
www.marywood.edu

Penn State
www.psu.edu

Abington Campus
Abington, PA
www.abington.psu.edu

Altoona Campus
Altoona, PA
www.aa.psu.edu

Beaver Campus
Monaca, PA
www.br.psu.edu

Berks Campus
Reading, PA
www.bk.psu.edu

Brandywine Campus
Media, PA
www.brandywine.psu.edu

DuBois Campus
DuBois, PA
www.ds.psu.edu

Erie, The Behrend College Campus
Erie, PA
www.erie.psu.edu

Fayette, The Eberly Campus
Uniontown, PA
www.fe.psu.edu

Greater Allegheny Campus
McKeesport, PA
www.ga.psu.edu

Hazleton Campus
Hazleton, PA
www.hn.psu.edu

Lehigh Valley Campus
Fogelsville, PA
www.lv.psu.edu

Mont Alto Campus
Mont Alto, PA
www.ma.psu.edu

New Kensington Campus
New Kensington, PA
www.nk.psu.edu

Schuylkill Campus
Schuylkill Haven, PA
www.sl.psu.edu

Shenango Campus
Sharon, PA
www.shenango.psu.edu

University Park (Main Campus)*
University Park, PA
www.psu.edu

Wilkes-Barre Campus
Lehman, PA
www.wb.psu.edu

Worthington Scranton Campus
Dunmore, PA
www.sn.psu.edu

York Campus
York, PA
www.yk.psu.edu

Point Park University
Pittsburgh, PA
www.pointpark.edu

University of Pittsburgh
Bradford Campus
Bradford, PA
www.upb.pitt.edu

Greensburg Campus
Greensburg, PA
www.upg.pitt.edu

Villanova University
Villanova, PA
www.villanova.edu

Waynesburg University
Waynesburg, PA
www.waynesburg.edu

York College of Pennsylvania
York, PA
www.ycp.edu

Puerto Rico

Interamerican University of Puerto Rico
www.inter.edu

Barranquitas Campus
Barranquitas, PR
www.br.inter.edu

Guayama Campus
Guayama, PR
www.guayama.inter.edu

Ponce Campus
Ponce, PR
www.ponce.inter.edu

Universidad Metropolitana
Cupey, PR
www.suagm.edu

Universidad del Este
Carolina, PR
www.suagm.edu

University of Puerto Rico, Carolina
Regional College
Carolina, PR
www.uprc.edu

Rhode Island

Johnson & Wales University, Providence
Providence, RI
www.jwu.edu

Roger Williams University
Bristol, RI
www.rwu.edu

Salve Regina University
Newport, RI
www.salve.edu

South Carolina

Anderson University
Anderson, SC
www.andersonuniversity.edu

The Citadel, The Military College of South Carolina
Charleston, SC
www.citadel.edu

Claflin University
Orangeburg, SC
www.claflin.edu

Limestone College
Gaffney, SC
www.limestone.edu

Morris College
Sumter, SC
www.morris.edu

South Carolina State University
Orangeburg, SC
www.scsu.edu

South University
Columbia, SC
www.southuniversity.edu

University of South Carolina*
Columbia, SC
www.sc.edu

South Dakota

None that offer BA degrees

Tennessee

Austin Peay State University
Clarksville, TN
www.apsu.edu

East Tennessee State University
Johnson City, TN
www.etsu.edu

Lambuth University
Jackson, TN
www.lambuth.edu

Middle Tennessee State University
Murfreesboro, TN
www.mtsu.edu

University of Memphis
Memphis, TN
www.memphis.edu

University of Tennessee
Chattanooga Campus
Chattanooga, TN
www.utc.edu

Martin Campus
Martin, TN
www.utm.edu

Texas

Abilene Christian University
Abilene, TX
www.acu.edu

Concordia University at Austin
Austin, TX
www.concordia.edu

Lubbock Christian University
Lubbock, TX
www.lcu.edu

Texas A&M University, Commerce
College Station, TX
www.tamu.edu

Texas College
Tyler, TX
www.texascollege.edu

Texas Southern University
Houston, TX
www.tsu.edu

University of Houston-Victoria
Victoria, TX
www.uhv.edu

University of Mary Hardin-Baylor
Belton, TX
www.umhb.edu

University of Texas
Brownsville Campus
Brownsville, TX
www.utb.edu

Pan American Campus
Edinburg, TX
www.utpa.edu

West Texas A&M University
Canyon, TX
www.wtamu.edu

Wiley College
Marshall, TX
www.wileyc.edu

Utah

Utah Valley University (formerly Utah Valley State College)
Orem, UT
www.uvu.edu

Vermont

None that offer BA degrees

Virginia

Averett University
Danville, VA
www.averett.edu

Bluefield College
Bluefield, VA
www.bluefield.edu

Hampton University*
Hampton, VA
www.hampton.edu

Virginia Commonwealth University
Richmond, VA
www.vcu.edu

Virginia Intermont College
Bristol, VA
www.vic.edu

Washington

None that offer BA degrees

West Virginia

American Public University System
Charles Town, WV
www.apus.edu

Fairmont State University
Fairmont, WV
www.fairmontstate.edu

Mountain State University
(formerly called The College of West Virginia)
Beckley, WV
www.mountainstate.edu

West Virginia Wesleyan College
Buckhannon, WV
www.wvwc.edu

Wisconsin

Lakeland College
Sheboygan, WI
www.lakeland.edu

Marian College of Fond du Lac
Fond du Lac, WI
www.mariancollege.edu

University of Wisconsin, Platteville
Platteville, WI
www.uwplatt.edu

Wyoming

None that offer BA degrees

Appendix B

Colleges and Universities That Offer Four-year Bachelor's Degrees in Criminal Justice Studies[1]

Listed alphabetically by state and then by college or university

Alabama

Alabama State University
Montgomery, AL
www.alasu.edu

Andrew Jackson University
Birmingham, AL
www.aju.edu

Athens State University
Athens, AL
www.athens.edu

Auburn University at Montgomery
Montgomery, AL
www.aum.edu

Faulkner University
Montgomery, AL
www.faulkner.edu

Jacksonville State University
Jacksonville, AL
www.jsu.edu

Troy University
Troy, AL
www.troy.edu

University of Alabama
Tuscaloosa, AL
www.ua.edu

University of Alabama, Birmingham
Birmingham, AL
www.uab.edu

University of South Alabama
Mobile, AL
www.usouthal.edu

An * denotes a college included in *The Best 366 Colleges, 2008 Edition*, published by The Princeton Review.

Alaska

University of Alaska, Fairbanks
Fairbanks, AK
www.uaf.edu

Arizona

Arizona State University*
Tempe, AZ
www.asu.edu

Everest College, Phoenix
Phoenix, AZ
www.everest.edu

Grand Canyon University
Phoenix, AZ
www.gcu.edu

Northern Arizona University
Flagstaff, AZ
www.nau.edu

University of Phoenix
Phoenix, AZ
www.phoenix.edu

Arkansas

Harding University
Searcy, AR
www.harding.edu

Southern Arkansas University
Magnolia, AR
www.saumag.edu

University of Arkansas
www.uark.edu

Little Rock Campus
Little Rock, AR
www.ualr.edu

Monticello Campus
Monticello, AR
www.uamont.edu

Pine Bluff Campus
Pine Bluff, AR
www.uapb.edu

California

California State University
www.calstate.edu

Bakersfield Campus
Bakersfield, CA
www.csub.edu

Chico Campus
Chico, CA
www.csuchico.edu

Fullerton Campus
Fullerton, CA
www.fullerton.edu

Long Beach Campus
Long Beach, CA
www.csulb.edu

Sacramento Campus
Sacramento, CA
www.csus.edu

Stanislaus Campus*
Turlock, CA
www.csustan.edu

National University
San Diego, CA
www.nu.edu

San Francisco State University
San Francisco, CA
www.sfsu.edu

San Jose State University
San Jose, CA
www.sjsu.edu

Westwood College: South Bay
Torrance, CA
www.westwood.edu

Colorado

Mesa State College
Grand Junction, CO
www.mesastate.edu

Metropolitan State College of Denver
Denver, CO
www.mscd.edu

Remington College, Colorado Springs
Colorado Springs, CO
www.remingtoncollege.edu

University of Northern Colorado
Greeley, CO
www.univnorthco.edu

Western State College of Colorado
Gunnison, CO
www.western.edu

Connecticut

Albertus Magnus College
New Haven, CT
www.albertus.edu

Briarwood College
Southington, CT
www.briarwood.edu

Quinnipiac University*
Hamden, CT
www.quinnipiac.edu

Delaware

Delaware State University
Dover, DE
www.desu.edu

University of Delaware
Newark, DE
www.udel.edu

Wilmington University
New Castle, DE
www.wilmu.edu

District of Columbia

American University*
Washington, D.C.
www.american.edu

George Washington University*
Washington, D.C.
www.gwu.edu

Florida

Everest University (formerly Florida Metropolitan University, or FMU)
Lakeland Campus
Lakeland, FL
www.everest.edu

Tampa Campus
Tampa, FL
www.fmu.edu

Florida Agricultural and Mechanical University
Tallahassee, FL
www.famu.edu

Florida Atlantic University
Boca Raton, FL (and other locations)
www.fau.edu

Florida Gulf Coast University
Fort Myers, FL
www.fgcu.edu

Florida International University
Miami, FL
www.fiu.edu

Hodges University
Naples and Ft. Myers, FL
www.hodges.edu

Miami Dade College
Homestead, FL
www.mdc.edu

Nova Southeastern University
Ft. Lauderdale and Davie, FL
www.nova.edu

Remington College, Largo
Largo, FL
www.remingtoncollege.edu

St. Leo University
Saint Leo, FL
www.saintleo.edu

Saint Thomas University
Miami Gardens, FL
www.stu.edu

Southwest Florida College
Ft. Myers and Tampa, FL
www.swfc.edu

University of Central Florida*
Orlando, FL
www.ucf.edu

University of North Florida
Jacksonville, FL
www.unf.edu

University of South Florida*
Tampa, FL (and other Campuses)
www.usf.edu

University of West Florida
Pensacola, FL
www.uwf.edu

Georgia

Albany State University
Albany, GA
www.asurams.edu

Ashworth University
Norcross, GA
www.ashworthuniversity.edu

Augusta State University
Augusta, GA
www.aug.edu

Clark Atlanta University
Atlanta, GA
www.cau.edu

Columbus State University
Columbus, GA
www.colstate.edu

Georgia Southern University
Statesboro, GA
www.georgiasouthern.edu

Georgia State University
Atlanta, GA
www.gsu.edu

Kennesaw State University
Kennesaw, GA
www.kennesaw.edu

Mercer University
Macon, GA
www.mercer.edu

Piedmont College
Demorest Athens, GA
www.piedmont.edu

Thomas University
Thomasville, GA
www.thomasu.edu

University of Georgia*
Athens, GA
www.uga.edu

Valdosta State University
Valdosta, GA
www.valdosta.edu

Hawaii

Remington College, Honolulu
Honolulu, HI
www.remingtoncollege.edu

Idaho

Lewis-Clark State College
Lewiston, ID
www.lcsc.edu

University of Idaho*
Moscow, ID
www.uidaho.edu

Illinois

Aurora University
Aurora, IL
www.aurora.edu

Blackburn College
Carlinville, IL
www.blackburn.edu

Concordia University
Chicago, IL
www.cuchicago.edu

Governors State University
University Park, IL
www.govst.edu

Illinois State University
Normal, IL
www.ilstu.edu

Lewis University
Romeoville, IL
www.lewisu.edu

Loyola University Chicago*
Chicago, IL
www.luc.edu

Northeastern Illinois University
Chicago, IL
www.neiu.edu

Olivet Nazarene University
Bourbonnais, IL
www.olivet.edu

Quincy University
Quincy, IL
www.quincy.edu

Roosevelt University
Chicago, IL
www.roosevelt.edu

St. Xavier University
Chicago, IL
www.sxu.edu

Southern Illinois University, Edwardsville
Edwardsville, IL
www.siue.edu

University of Illinois
www.uillinois.edu

Chicago Campus
Chicago, IL
www.uic.edu

Springfield Campus
Springfield, IL
www.uis.ed

Westwood College of Technology
DuPage Campus
Woodridge, IL
www.westwood.edu

O'Hare Airport Campus
Chicago, IL
www.westwood.edu

Indiana

Anderson University
Anderson, IN
www.anderson.edu

Ball State University
Muncie, IN
http://cms.bsu.edu

Butler University
Indianapolis, IN
www.butler.edu

Grace College
Winona Lake, IN
www.grace.edu

Indiana Institute of Technology
Fort Wayne, IN (Main Campus)
www.indianatech.edu

Indiana University
Bloomington Campus*
Bloomington, IN
www.iub.edu

East Campus
Richmond, IN
www.iue.edu

Kokomo Campus
Kokomo, IN
www.iuk.edu

Northwest Campus
Gary, IN
www.iun.edu

South Bend Campus
South Bend, IN
www.iusb.edu

Indiana University-Purdue University, Indianapolis
Indianapolis, IN
www.iupui.edu

Indiana Wesleyan University
Marion, IN
www.indwes.edu

Oakland City University
Bedford, IN
www.oak.edu

Saint Joseph's College
Rensselaer, IN
www.saintjoe.edu

Taylor University Fort Wayne
Fort Wayne, IN
www.fw.taylor.edu

Trine University (formerly known as Tri-State University)
Angola, IN
www.tristate.edu

Iowa

Buena Vista University
Storm Lake, IA
www.bvu.edu

Graceland University
Lamoni, IA
www.graceland.edu

Grand View College
Des Moines, IA
www.gvc.edu

Iowa Wesleyan College
Mount Pleasant, IA
www.iwc.edu

Kaplan University, Davenport
Davenport, IA
www.kuCampus.edu

Loras College
Dubuque, IA
www.loras.edu

St. Ambrose University
Davenport, IA
www.sau.edu

Simpson College
Indianola, IA
www.simpson.edu

University of Dubuque
Dubuque, IA
www.dbq.edu

Upper Iowa University
Fayette, IA
www.uiu.edu

William Penn University
Oskaloosa, IA
www.wmpenn.edu

Kansas

Bethany College
Lindsborg, KS
www.bethanylb.edu

Fort Hays State University
Hays, KS
www.fhsu.edu

Kansas Wesleyan University
Salina, KS
www.kwu.edu

Southwestern College
Winfield, KS
www.sckans.edu

Washburn University
Topeka, KS
www.washburn.edu

Wichita State University
Wichita, KS
www.wichita.edu

Kentucky

Kentucky State University
Frankfort, KY
www.kysu.edu

Kentucky Wesleyan College
Owensboro, KY
www.kwc.edu

Lindsey Wilson College
Columbia, KY
www.lindsey.edu

Murray State University
Murray, KY
www.murraystate.edu

Northern Kentucky University
Highland Heights, KY
www.nku.edu

Pikeville College
Pikeville, KY
www.pc.edu

Louisiana

Grambling State University
Grambling, LA
www.gram.edu

Louisiana State University,* Shreveport
Shreveport, LA
www.lsus.edu

Loyola University New Orleans*
New Orleans, LA
www.loyno.edu

McNeese State University
Lake Charles, LA
www.mcneese.edu

Southeastern Louisiana University
Hammond, LA
www.selu.edu

Southern University, New Orleans
New Orleans, LA
www.suno.edu

Southern University and A&M College
Baton Rouge, LA
www.subr.edu

University of Louisiana, Lafayette*
Lafayette, LA
www.louisiana.edu

University of Louisiana, Monroe
Monroe, LA
www.nlu.edu

Maine

Husson College
Bangor, ME
www.husson.edu

St. Joseph's College
Standish, ME
www.sjcme.edu

Thomas College
Waterville, ME
www.thomas.edu

Maryland

Coppin State University
Baltimore, MD
www.coppin.edu

Mount St. Mary's University
Emmitsburg, MD
www.msmary.edu

University of Baltimore
Baltimore, MD
www.ubalt.edu

Massachusetts

American International College
Springfield, MA
www.aic.edu

Anna Maria College
Paxton, MA
www.annamaria.edu

Bay Path College
Longmeadow, MA
www.baypath.edu

Becker College
Worcester, MA
www.becker.edu

Bridgewater State College
Bridgewater, MA
www.bridgew.edu

Curry College
Milton, MA
www.curry.edu

Endicott College
Beverly, MA
www.endicott.edu

Fitchburg State College
Fitchburg, MA
www.fsc.edu

Mount Ida College
Newton, MA
www.mountida.edu

Nichols College
Dudley, MA
www.nichols.edu

Northeastern University*
Boston, MA
www.neu.edu

University of Massachusetts, Boston
Boston, MA
www.bu.edu

Western New England College
Springfield, MA
www.wnec.edu

Westfield State College
Westfield, MA
www.wsc.mass.edu

Worcester State College
Worcester, MA
www.worcester.edu

Michigan

Adrian College
Adrian, MI
www.adrian.edu

Madonna University
Livonia, MI
www.madonna.edu

Michigan State University*
East Lansing, MI
www.msu.edu

Northern Michigan University
Marquette, MI
www.nmu.edu

Olivet College
Olivet, MI
www.olivetcollege.edu

Saginaw Valley State University
Saginaw, MI
www.svsu.edu

Siena Heights University
Adrian, MI
www.sienaheights.edu

University of Detroit Mercy
Detroit, MI
www.udmercy.edu

Wayne State University
Detroit, MI
www.wayne.edu

Western Michigan University
Kalamazoo, MI
www.wmich.edu

Minnesota

Bemidji State University
Bemidji, MN
www.bemidjistate.edu

Brown College
Mendota Heights, MN
www.browncollege.edu

Concordia University, St. Paul
St. Paul, MN
www.csp.edu

Gustavus Adolphus College*
Saint Peter, MN
www.gustavus.edu

Hamline University
Saint Paul, MN
www.hamline.edu

Metropolitan State University
St. Paul, MN
www.metrostate.edu

Minnesota State University, Moorhead
Moorhead, MN
www.mnstate.edu

Northwestern College
St. Paul, MN
www.nwc.edu

Saint Cloud State University
St. Cloud, MN
www.stcloudstate.edu

St. Mary's University of Minnesota
Minneapolis, MN
www.smumn.edu

Winona State University
Winona MN
www.winona.edu

Mississippi

Alcorn State University
Lorman, MS
www.alcorn.edu

Delta State University
Cleveland, MS
www.deltastate.edu

Jackson State University
Jackson, MS
www.jsums.edu

Mississippi Valley State University
Itta Bena, MS
www.mvsu.edu

University of Southern Mississippi
Hattiesburg, MS
www.usm.edu

Missouri

Evangel University
Springfield, MO
www.evangel.edu

Lindenwood University
St. Charles, MO
www.lindenwood.edu

Missouri Baptist University
St. Louis, MO
www.mobap.edu

Missouri Western State University
St. Joseph, MO
www.missouriwestern.edu

Truman State University*
Kirksville, MO
www.truman.edu

Montana

Montana State University, Billings
Billings, MT
www.msubillings.edu

University of Great Falls
Great Falls, MT
www.ugf.edu

Nebraska

University of Nebraska
Lincoln, NE (Main Campus)
www.unl.edu

Kearney Campus
Kearney, NE
www.unk.edu

Omaha Campus
Omaha, NE
www.unomaha.edu

Wayne State College
Wayne, NE
www.wsc.edu

Nevada

None that offer BA degrees

New Hampshire

Franklin Pierce University
Rindge, NH
www.franklinpierce.edu

Granite State College
Concord, NH
www.granite.edu

New England College
Henniker, NH
www.nec.edu

Plymouth State University
Plymouth, NH
www.plymouth.edu

St. Anselm College*
Manchester, NH
www.anselm.edu

New Jersey

Caldwell College
Caldwell, NJ
www.caldwell.edu

Centenary College
Hackettstown, NJ
www.centenarycollege.edu

Fairleigh Dickinson University,
Metropolitan Campus
Teaneck, NH
www.fdu.edu

Monmouth University*
West Long Branch, NJ
www.monmouth.edu

Rowan University
Glassboro, NJ
www.rowan.edu

Rutgers, The State University of
New Jersey
www.rutgers.edu
Camden Regional Campus
Camden, NJ
www.camden.rutgers.edu

Newark Regional Campus
Newark, NJ
www.rutgers-newark.rutgers.edu

Seton Hall University*
South Orange, NJ
www.shu.edu

Thomas Edison State College
Trenton, NJ
www.tesc.edu

New Mexico

University of the Southwest
Hobbs, NM
www.usw.edu

Eastern New Mexico University
Portales, NM
www.enmu.edu

New Mexico Highlands University
Las Vegas, NM
www.nmhu.edu

New Mexico State University
Las Cruces, NM
www.nmsu.edu

Western New Mexico University
Silver City, NM
www.wnmu.edu

New York

Alfred University*
Alfred, NY
www.alfred.edu

Berkeley College of New York City
New York, NY
www.berkeleycollege.edu

Canisius College
Buffalo, NY
www.canisius.edu

Cazenovia College
Cazenovia, NY
www.cazenovia.edu

Elmira College
Elmira, NY
www.elmira.edu

Excelsior College
Albany, NY
www.excelsior.edu

Fordham University*
Bronx, NY
www.fordham.edu

Hilbert College
Hamburg, NY
www.hilbert.edu

Niagara University
Niagara University, NY
www.niagara.edu

Russell Sage College
Troy and Albany, NY
www.sage.edu/rsc

St. Francis College
Brooklyn Heights, NY
www.stfranciscollege.edu

State University of New York
www.suny.edu

Albany Campus*
Albany, NY
www.albany.edu

College at Buffalo*
Buffalo, NY
www.buffalo.edu

College at Fredonia
Fredonia, NY
www.fredonia.edu

College at Oneonta
Oneonta, NY
www.oneonta.edu

College at Plattsburgh
Plattsburgh, NY
www.plattsburgh.edu

College at Potsdam
Potsdam, NY
www.potsdam.edu

Institute of Technology at Utica/Rome
Utica, NY
www.sunyit.edu

Utica College
Utica, NY
www.utica.edu

North Carolina

Appalachian State University
Boone, NC
www.appstate.edu

Barton College
Wilson, NC
www.barton.edu

Belmont Abbey College
Belmont, NC
www.belmontabbeycollege.edu

Campbell University
Buies Creek, NC
www.campbell.edu

East Carolina University
Greenville, NC
www.ecu.edu

Elizabeth City State University
Elizabeth City, NC
www.ecsu.edu

Elon University*
Elon, NC
www.elon.edu

Fayetteville State University
Fayetteville, NC
www.uncfsu.edu

Guilford College*
Greensboro, NC
www.guilford.edu

High Point University
High Point, NC
www.highpoint.edu

Lees-McRae College
Banner Elk, NC
www.lmc.edu

Livingstone College
Salisbury, NC
www.livingstone.edu

Methodist University
Fayetteville, NC
www.methodist.edu

Mount Olive College
Greensboro, NC
www.moc.edu

North Carolina Wesleyan College
Rocky Mount, NC
www.ncwc.edu

Pfeiffer University
Misenheimer, NC
www.pfeiffer.edu

St. Augustine's College
Raleigh, NC
www.st-aug.edu

Shaw University
Raleigh, NC
www.shawuniversity.edu

University of North Carolina
www.northcarolina.edu

Charlotte Campus
Charlotte, NC
www.unnc.edu

Pembroke Campus
Pembroke, NC
www.uncp.edu

Wilmington Campus
Wilmington, NC
www.uncwil.edu

Western Carolina University
Cullowhee, NC
www.wcu.edu

Winston-Salem State University
Winston Salem, NC
www.wssu.edu

North Dakota

Jamestown College
Jamestown, ND
www.jc.edu

Minot State University
Minot, ND
www.minotstateu.edu

North Dakota State University
Fargo, ND
www.ndsu.edu

University of Mary
Bismarck, ND
www.umary.edu

University of North Dakota*
Grand Forks, ND
www.und.edu

Ohio

Baldwin-Wallace College
Berea, OH
www.bw.edu

Bluffton University
Bluffton, OH
www.bluffton.edu

Bowling Green State University
Bowling Green, OH
www.bgsu.edu

Central State University
Wilberforce, OH
www.centralstate.edu

Kent State University
Kent, OH
www.kent.edu

Lourdes College
Sylvania, OH
www.lourdes.edu

Mount Vernon Nazarene University
Mount Vernon, OH
www.mvnu.edu

Ohio Dominican University
Columbus, OH
www.ohiodominican.edu

Ohio Northern University*
Ada, OH
www.onu.edu

Ohio University
www.ohio.edu
- Chillicothe Campus
  Chillicothe, OH
  www.chillicothe.ohiou.edu

Southern Campus, Ironton
Ironton, OH
www.southern.ohiou.edu

Union Institute & University
Cincinnati, OH
www.tui.edu

University of Akron
Akron, OH
www.uakron.edu

University of Cincinnati*
Cincinnati, OH
www.uc.edu

University of Dayton*
Dayton, OH
www.udayton.edu

University of Toledo
Toledo, OH
www.utoledo.edu

Urbana University
Urbana, OH
www.urbana.edu

Xavier University*
Cincinnati, OH
www.xavier.edu

Youngstown State University
Youngstown, OH
www.ysu.edu

Oklahoma

Cameron University
Duncan, OK
www.cameron.edu

East Central University
Ada, OK
www.ecok.edu

Southeastern Oklahoma State University
Durant, OK
www.sosu.edu

Southwestern Oklahoma State University
Weatherford, OK
www.swosu.edu

University of Central Oklahoma
Edmond, OK
www.ucok.edu

Oregon

Pioneer Pacific College
Wilsonville, OR (Main Campus)
www.pioneerpacificcollege.edu

Portland State University
Portland, OR
www.pdx.edu

Southern Oregon University
Ashland, OR
www.sou.edu

Pennsylvania

Bloomsburg University of
Pennsylvania
Bloomsburg, PA
www.bloomu.edu

California University of Pennsylvania
California, PA
www.cup.edu

Central Pennsylvania College
Summerdale, PA
www.centralpenn.edu

DeSales University
Center Valley, PA
www.desales.edu

Edinboro University of Pennsylvania
Edinboro, PA
www.edinboro.edu

Gannon University
Erie, PA
www.gannon.edu

Holy Family University
Philadelphia, PA
www.holyfamily.edu

Immaculata University
Immaculata, PA
www.immaculata.edu

Keystone College
La Plume, PA
www.keystone.edu

King's College
Wilkes-Barre, PA
www.kings.edu

Kutztown University of Pennsylvania
Kutztown, PA
www.kutztown.edu

La Roche College
Pittsburgh, PA
www.laroche.edu

La Salle University
Philadelphia, PA
www.lasalle.edu

Lincoln University
Lincoln University, PA
www.lincoln.edu

Lycoming College
Williamsport, PA
www.lycoming.edu

Mercyhurst College
Erie, PA
www.mercyhurst.edu

Messiah College
Grantham, PA
www.messiah.edu

Moravian College*
Bethlehem, PA
www.moravian.edu

Mount Aloysius College
Cresson, PA
www.mtaloy.edu

Neumann College
Aston, PA
www.neumann.edu

Penn State
www.psu.edu

Abington Campus
Abington, PA
www.abington.psu.edu

Altoona Campus
Altoona, PA
www.aa.psu.edu

Beaver Campus
Monaca, PA
www.br.psu.edu

Berks Campus
Reading, PA
www.bk.psu.edu

Brandywine Campus
Media, PA
www.brandywine.edu

DuBois Campus
DuBois, PA
www.ds.psu.edu

Erie, The Behrend College Campus
Erie, PA
www.erie.psu.edu

Fayette, The Eberly Campus
Uniontown, PA
www.fe.psu.edu

Greater Allegheny Campus
McKeesport, PA
www.ga.psu.edu

Harrisburg Campus
Harrisburg, PA
www.hbg.psu.edu

Hazleton Campus
Hazleton, PA
www.hn.psu.edu

Lehigh Valley Campus
Foglesville, PA
www.lv.psu.edu

Mont Alto Campus
Mont Alto, PA
www.ma.psu.edu

New Kensington Campus
New Kensington, PA
www.nk.psu.edu

Schuylkill Campus
Schuylkill Haven, PA
www.sl.psu.edu

Shenango Campus
Sharon, PA
www.shenango.edu

Wilkes-Barre Campus
Lehman, PA
www.wb.psu.edu

Worthington Scranton Campus
Dunmore, PA
www.sn.psu.edu

York Campus
York, PA
www.yk.psu.edu

Point Park University
Pittsburgh, PA
www.pointpark.edu

Rosemont College
Rosemont, PA
www.rosemont.edu

Seton Hill University
Greensburg, PA
www.setonhill.edu

Shippensburg University
Shippensburg, PA
www.ship.edu

Temple University*
Philadelphia, PA
www.temple.edu

Thiel College
Greenville, PA
www.thiel.edu

University of Scranton*
Scranton, PA
www.scranton.edu

West Chester University of Pennsylvania
West Chester, PA
www.wcupa.edu

Westminster College*
New Wilmington, PA
www.westminster.edu

Wilkes University
Wilkes-Barre, PA
www.wilkes.edu

Puerto Rico

Interamerican University of Puerto Rico

Aguadilla Campus
Aguadilla, PR
www.aguadilla.inter.edu

Arecibo Campus
Arecibo, PR
www.arecibo.inter.edu

Fajardo Campus
Fajardo, PR
www.fajardo.inter.edu

Metro Campus
Rio Piedras, PR
www.metro.inter.edu

Universidad Metropolitana
Cupey, PR
www.suagm.edu

Rhode Island

Rhode Island College
Providence, RI
www.ric.edu

South Carolina

Charleston Southern University
Charleston, SC
www.csuniv.edu

Southern Wesleyan University
Central, SC
www.swu.edu

University of South Carolina Upstate
Spartanburg, SC
www.uscupstate.edu

South Dakota

Dakota Wesleyan University
Mitchell, SD
www.dwu.edu

Mount Marty College
Yankton, SD
www.mtmc.edu

University of South Dakota*
Vermillion, SD
www.usd.edu

Tennessee

Cumberland University
Lebanon, TN
www.cumberland.edu

Freed-Hardeman University
Henderson, TN
www.fhu.edu

Lane College
Jackson, TN
www.lanecollege.edu

Tennessee State University
Nashville, TN
www.tnstate.edu

University of Tennessee, Knoxville*
Knoxville, TN
www.utk.edu

Texas

Angelo State University
San Angelo, TX
www.angelo.edu

Dallas Baptist University
Dallas, TX
www.dbu.edu

Hardin-Simmons University
Abilene, TX
www.hsutx.edu

Huston-Tillotson University
Austin, TX
www.htu.edu

Jarvis Christian College
Hawkins, TX
www.jarvis.edu

Lamar University
Beaumont, TX
www.lamar.edu

Midwestern State University
Wichita Falls, TX
www.mwsu.edu

Our Lady of the Lake University
San Antonio, TX
www.ollusa.edu

Prairie View A&M University
Prairie View, TX
www.pvamu.edu

St. Edward's University
Austin, TX
www.stedwards.edu

St. Mary's University
San Antonio, TX
www.stmarytx.edu

Sam Houston State University
Huntsville, TX
www.shsu.edu

Southwestern Adventist University
Keene, TX
www.swau.edu

Stephen F. Austin State University
Nacogdoches, TX
www.sfasu.edu

Sul Ross State University
Alpine, TX
www.sulross.edu

Tarleton State University
Stephenville, TX
www.tarleton.edu

Texas A&M University
www.tamu.edu

Commerce Campus
Commerce, TX
www.tamu-commerce.edu

Texarkana Campus
Texarkana, TX
www.tamut.edu

Texas Christian University*
Fort Worth, TX
www.tcu.edu

Texas State University, San Marcos
San Marcos, TX
www.txstate.edu

Texas Woman's University
Denton, TX (and other Campuses)
www.twu.edu

University of Houston, Downtown
Houston, TX
www.uhd.edu

University of Texas

Arlington Campus
Arlington, TX
www.uta.edu

El Paso Campus
El Paso, TX
www.utep.edu

San Antonio Campus
San Antonio, TX
www.utsa.edu

Tyler Campus
Tyler, TX
www.uttyler.edu

Permian Basin Campus
Odessa, TX
www.utpb.edu

Wayland Baptist University
Plainview, TX
www.wbu.edu

Utah

Southern Utah University
Cedar City, UT
www.suu.edu

Weber State University
Ogden, UT
www.weber.edu

Vermont

Castleton State College
Castleton, VT
www.csc.vsc.edu

Champlain College
Burlington, VT
www.champlain.edu

Norwich University
Northfield, VT
www.norwich.edu

Virginia

Ferrum College
Ferrum, VA
www.ferrum.edu

Liberty University
Lynchburg, VA
www.liberty.edu

Longwood University
Farmville, VA
www.longwood.edu

Marymount University
Arlington, VA
www.marymount.edu

Radford University
Radford, VA
www.runet.edu

Roanoke College
Salem, VA
www.roanoke.edu

St. Paul's College
Lawrenceville, VA
www.saintpauls.edu

University of Richmond*
Richmond, VA
www.richmond.edu

University of Virginia's College at Wise
Wise, VA
www.wise.virginia.edu

Virginia Wesleyan College
Norfolk, VA
www.vwc.edu

Washington

Central Washington University
Ellensburg, WA
www.cwu.edu

Gonzaga University*
Spokane, WA
www.gonzaga.edu

Saint Martin's University
Lacey, WA
www.stmartin.edu

Seattle University*
Seattle, WA
www.seattleu.edu

West Virginia

Bluefield State College
Bluefield, WV (and other Campuses)
www.bluefieldstate.edu

Fairmont State University
Fairmont, WV
www.fairmontstate.edu

Marshall University
Huntington, WV
www.marshall.edu

Mountain State University (formerly The College of West Virginia)
Beckley, WV (and other Campuses)
www.mountainstate.edu

Salem International University
Salem, WV
www.salemu.edu

West Liberty State College
West Liberty, WV
www.westliberty.edu

Wheeling Jesuit University
Wheeling, WV
www.wju.edu

Wisconsin

Carroll College
Waukesha, WI
www.cc.edu

Concordia University Wisconsin
Mequon, WI
www.cuw.edu

Edgewood College
Madison, WI
www.edgewood.edu

Mount Mary College
Milwaukee, WI
www.mtmary.edu

University of Wisconsin
www.uwsa.edu

Eau Claire Campus
Eau Claire, WI
www.uwec.edu

Madison Campus*
Madison, WI
www.wisc.edu

Milwaukee Campus
Milwaukee, WI
www.uwm.edu

Parkside Campus
Kenosha, WI
www.uwp.edu

Superior Campus
Superior, WI
www.uwsuper.edu

Viterbo University
La Crosse, WI
www.viterbo.edu

Wyoming

University of Wyoming*
Laramie, WY
www.uwyo.edu

Appendix C

Additional Sources of Information: Websites and Print Resources

WEBSITES

www.cpb.gov
The website of the U.S. Customs and Border Protection Agency.

www.dhs.gov
The Department of Homeland Security website.

www.opm.gov
The Office of Personnel Management website.

www.opm.gov/veterans
Information for veterans.

https://cbpmhc.hr-services.org/BPA
Visit this site to check for open positions in the Border Patrol.

https://cbpmhc.hr-services.org/BPA/
See this site for the online application to become a Border Patrol Agent.

www.cbp.gov/xp/cgov/careers/customs_careers/border_careers/fitness_requirements
Log onto this website for a detailed explanation of the proper form for each of these three pre-employment fitness tests you will be required to take. (This website also links to a 17-minute audio presentation that describes each test in detail and then gives you time to practice each test as it will actually be administered.)

http://www.dhs.gov/xabout/careers/

This site provides information on other careers within the Department of Homeland Security (in addition to that of Border Patrol Agent, if you decide that the CBP is not the right agency for you).

www.dol.gov/elaws/vets/vetpref/mservice.htm

Visit this website to determine if you are eligible for a veterans' preference. (This site will ask you a series of questions, at the end of which it will calculate how many points you may have toward your score for when you apply and are tested for nonmilitary law-enforcement jobs, such as Border Patrol Agent.)

www.honorfirst.com

This is an unofficial Border Patrol recruiting website, managed by a highly regarded former Border Patrol Agent. (Current and former Border Patrol Agents recommend this site because it consolidates real-world information regarding testing, positions, academy schedules, and pay and benefits, and even includes an online message board, moderated by active Border Patrol Agents, to talk to real agents or with other applicants.)

www.nbpc1613.org

This is the official website of the largest Border Patrol Agents Association (National Border Patrol Council Local 1613, San Diego, CA). It provides information on the latest workplace issues affecting Border Patrol Agents, pay, legislation, and general inside information regarding the work of agents.

www.opm.gov/qualifications/SEC-II/s2-e5.asp

This site provides detailed information on SAA, the Superior Academic Achievement requirement, to see if you might qualify to be hired at the GL-7 level instead of the GL-5 level of Border Patrol Agent.

www.tsa.gov/assets/pdf/soar/preparation_manual_bpa.pdf

This website offers a *Preparation Manual for the U.S. Border Patrol Test* you can download.

www.bpspouses.com

This free site managed by the spouse of a current Border Patrol Agent provides just about all information you would need regarding life as the spouse of a Border Patrol Agent.

PRINT RESOURCES

Preparation Manual for the U.S. Border Patrol Test, U.S. Department of Homeland Security/Customs and Border Protection.

Border Patrol Exam, Fourth Edition, New York: Learning Express, LLC, 2008.

Patrolling Chaos: The U.S. Border Patrol in Deep South Texas, Robert Lee Maril, Texas Tech University Press, 2006. This 368-page book focuses on one station, with 300 agents. Over a two-year period, it follows 12 typical agents, men and women, as they go about their regular 10-hour patrols along the border. It describes the daily challenges and risks they face and the perspectives and insights they hold as a result of their extensive, first-hand experience with the hard realities of immigration policy, the war on drugs, and the threat of terrorist infiltration. The author writes about the surveillance and apprehension of thousands of undocumented workers, drug interdictions involving huge quantities of marijuana and cocaine, the deaths of illegal immigrants by drowning and as a result of high-speed chases, corruption among law enforcers, and other events that shape the work lives of agents. The book also describes the impact of the 9/11 attacks on border security and on the personal lives of the Agents and their families.

The Closing of the American Border: Terrorism, Immigration, and Security since 9/11, Edward Alden, Harper, 2008. This book was written by the former Washington bureau chief of *The Financial Times* newspaper and was reviewed by *Publisher's Weekly* (a publishing trade magazine) as "a thoughtful and balanced assessment of border security and immigration policies before and after the terrorist attacks on September 11, 2001, demonstrating how more stringent security can damage the U.S. economy by discouraging trade, tourism and an influx of bright minds and diligent workers."

Border Patrol Agent: Test Preparation and Study Guide, Jack Rudman, National Learning Corp., 2001.

Endnotes

INTRODUCTION WHY YOU NEED THIS BOOK

1. "Border Patrol to hire 6,000 by end of 2008," Amanda Miller, www.armytimes.com/careers/second_careers/military_border-patrol_070530.
2. "Military.com Q&A with the U.S. Border Patrol," answer from Border Patrol Agent Noel Quinones, www.military.com/careers/content1?file=border_patrolqa.htm&area=Content.
3. Amanda Miller, op. cit.
4. Ibid.
5. Ibid.
6. "Military.com Q&A with the U.S. Border Patrol," answer from Border Patrol Agent Bruce Cooke, www.military.com/careers/content1?file=border_patrolqa.htm&area=Content.
7. Ibid.
8. "Border Patrol looks to military to fill ranks," Brady McCombs, *Arizona Daily Star*, May 25, 2007.
9. "Your Career as a Border Patrol Agent," www.cbp.gov/xp/cgov/careers/customs_careers/border_careers/bp_agent/.
10. Ibid.
11. Ibid.
12. "Border Patrol Academy expands," Jacques Belleaud, AP writer, www.navytimes.com.
13. Brady McCombs, op. cit.
14. Ibid.
15. "Border Patrol: 2,000 new agents the limit," Lara Jakes Jordan, AP, *Bakersfield Californian*, May 24, 2005, www.freerepublic.com.
16. "CBP Border Patrol Encourages Women, Minorities to Join," www.cbp.gov, July 9, 2007.

17. Timeline of Immigration to U.S. 1815-1950; www.ellisisland immigrants.org/ellis_island_immigrants.htm.
18. "Estimated number of illegal immigrants in U.S.," Pew Hispanic Center, www.cnn.com/interactive/us/0603/charts.immigration/content.1.html.
19. "Illegal immigrant population down," Stephen Dinan, *The Washington Times*, October 2, 2008.
20. "Number of illegal immigrants hits 12M," Stephen Ohlemacher, Breitbart.com, March 7, 2006.
21. Ibid.
22. "Illegal immigrants in the U.S.: How many are there?" Brad Knickerbocker, *The Christian Science Monitor*, May 16, 2006.
23. Lara Jakes Jordan, op. cit.

CHAPTER ONE THE BASICS OF THE JOB: DUTIES, SALARY, CAREER PATH, AND HIRING TIMELINE

1. "Military.com Q&A with the U.S. Border Patrol," answer from Bruce Cooke, op. cit.
2. Noel Quinones, op. cit.
3. "Border Patrol Academy Expands," Jacques Billeaud, quoting Eddie Ray II, www.navytimes.com/careers/second_careers/military_border_academy_070530.
4. Jacques Billeaud, op. cit., quoting David Narrance.
5. Jacques Billeaud, op. cit., about Mario Bedolla.
6. "Border Patrol Struggles to Keep Newly Hired Agents," Elliot Spagat, AP writer, 8/28/2008, http://www.officer.com/web/online/Homeland-Defense-and-Terror-News/Border-Patrol-Struggles-to-Keep-Newly-Hired-Agents/8$42953.
7. "FAQs—Working for Border Patrol," 5/29/08, www.cbp.gov/xp/cgov/careers/customs_careers/border_careers/bp_agent/faqs_working_for_the_usbp.xml.
8. "Key Duties and Responsibilities" of Border Patrol Agent, www.tsa.gov/join/benefits/soar/cbp/bpa.shtm.

9. Position Classification Standard for Border Patrol Agent Series, GS-1896," U.S. Office of Personnel Management, pages 3–4, www.opm.gov/fedclass/gs1896.pdf.
10. "New Border Patrol garb means business," Elliot Spagat, *USA Today*, 8/17/07.
11. http://jobsearch.usajobs.gov/getjob.asp?JobID=76225327&brd=3876&AVSDM=2008%2D10%2D01+09%3A02%3A52&q=Border+Patrol+Agent&sort=rv&vw=d&Logo=0&FedPub=Y&FedEmp=N&SUBMIT1.x=0&SUBMIT1.y.
12. http://jobsearch.usajobs.gov/getjob.asp?JobID=76225327&brd=3876&AVSDM=2008%2D10%2D01+09%3A02%3A52&q=Border+Patrol+Agent&sort=rv&vw=d&Logo=0&FedPub=Y&FedEmp=N&SUBMIT1.x=0&SUBMIT1.y=0&ss=0&TabNum=3&rc=2.
13. Position Classification Standard for Border Patrol Agent Series, GS-1896," op. cit., page 24.
14. http://jobsearch.usajobs.gov/getjob.asp?JobID=76225327&brd=3876&AVSDM=2008%2D10%2D01+09%3A02%3A52&q=Border+Patrol+Agent&sort=rv&vw=d&Logo=0&FedPub=Y&FedEmp=N&SUBMIT1.x=0&SUBMIT1.y.
15. Position Classification Standard for Border Patrol Agent Series, GS-1896," op. cit., page 27.
16. http://jobsearch.usajobs.gov/getjob.asp?JobID=76225327&brd=3876&AVSDM=2008%2D10%2D01+09%3A02%3A52&q=Border+Patrol+Agent&sort=rv&vw=d&Logo=0&FedPub=Y&FedEmp=N&SUBMIT1.x=0&SUBMIT1.y.
17. Position Classification Standard for Border Patrol Agent Series, GS-1896," op. cit., pages 29–30.
18. Position Classification Standard for Border Patrol Agent Series, GS-1896," op. cit., pages 36–37.

CHAPTER TWO THE SKILLS, PHYSICAL ABILITIES, AND EDUCATION YOU NEED

1. Brady McCombs, op. cit.
2. Amanda Miller, op. cit.
3. Ibid.
4. Brady McCombs, op. cit.

CHAPTER THREE MILITARY ADVANTAGE AND PREFERENCE TO VETERANS

1. "Border Patrol Recruiters Cross Ocean for First Time Seeking Job Applicants at Six U.S. Military Installations in Germany," news release, March 21, 2008, from www.cpb.gov/xp.cgov/newsroom/news_releases/archives/2008_news_releases/march_2008/03212008.xml.
2. Amanda Miller, op. cit.
3. "Military.com Q&A with the U.S. Border Patrol," answer from Bruce Cooke, op. cit.
4. "Take Your Pick: Defense Jobs on the Rise," by Heidi Russell Rafferty, June 14, 2008, globalsecurity.org Defense Jobs Career Center, http://globalsecurity.clearancejobs.com/news.php?articleID=47.
5. Amanda Miller, op. cit.
6. www.dol.gov/elaws/vets/vetpref/vetspref.htm.
7. "Military experience a plus at career fair," John Ferak, *Omaha World-Herald*, September 12, 2008.
8. "Border Patrol tries to lure retired troops," Mimi Hall, *USA Today*, April 13, 2008.
9. Border Patrol Recruiters Cross Ocean for First Time Seeking Job Applicants at Six U.S. Military Installations in Germany," op. cit.
10. Brady McCombs, op. cit.
11. Ibid.
12. Ibid.
13. Ibid.

CHAPTER FOUR THE APPLICATION PROCESS

1. "Military.com Q&A with the U.S. Border Patrol," answer from Bruce Cooke, op. cit.
2. "Basic Qualifications and Medical Requirements for Border Patrol Agents, 4/30/2008, http://www.cbp.gov/xp/cgov/careers/customs_careers/border_careers/application_process/basic_requirements_for_bp.xml.
3. Http://cryptome.org/irs-ci/36426.html#ss2: *Handbook 9.10 Administrative Databases and Software*, Chapter 2: Treasury Enforcement Communication System (TECS) and International Fugitive Notices.
4. Http://www.fas.org/irp/agency/doj/fbi/is/ncic.htm.

CHAPTER FIVE PREPARING FOR THE U.S. BORDER PATROL AGENT EXAM

1. *Preparation Manual for the U.S. Border Patrol Test*, U.S. Department of Homeland Security/Customs and Border Protection, page 19.

CHAPTER SIX A HISTORY OF THE U.S. BORDER PATROL

1. All of the information on the history of the Texas Rangers is derived from the Texas Department of Public Safety's web site: www.txdps.state.tx.us/director_staff/texas_rangers/.
2. "Fourteenth Amendment to the United States Constitution," Wikipedia, http://en.wikipedia.org/wiki/Fourteenth_Amendment_to_the_United_States_Constitution.
3. "U.S. Border Patrol—Protecting Our Sovereign Borders," www.cbp.gov/xp/cgov/about/history/bp_historcut.xml; "History of Immigration Laws," www.justia.com/immigration; "Timeline of U.S. Immigration Law," http://media.www.testcp8.com/media/storage/paper1226/news/2008/03/03/ImmigrationFeature.
4. "History of Immigration Laws," www.justia.com/immigration.

5. "About USCIS," USCIS official web site: www.uscis.gov/portal/site/uscis.
6. www.dhs.gov/xabout/history/editorial_0133.shtm.
7. www.dhs.gov/xabout/structure/.

APPENDIX A COLLEGES AND UNIVERSITIES THAT OFFER FOUR-YEAR BACHELOR'S DEGREES IN CRIMINAL JUSTICE AND LAW ENFORCEMENT

1. *The College Board Book of Majors*, 2009.

APPENDIX B COLLEGES AND UNIVERSITIES THAT OFFER FOUR-YEAR BACHELOR'S DEGREES IN CRIMINAL JUSTICE STUDIES

1. *The College Board Book of Majors*, 2009.